COLLOQUIUM:
Dilemmas of Academic Discourse

KAREN TRACY
University of Colorado

Ablex Publishing Corporation
Norwood, New Jersey

Printed in the United States of America

Tracy, Karen.
    Colloquium : dilemmas of academic discourse / Karen Tracy.
      p. cm. - - (Advances in discourse processes ; v. 60)
    Includes bibliographical references and index.
    ISBN 1-56750-223-7. - - ISBN 1-56750-224-5 (pbk.)
    1. Communication in small groups. 2. Discourse analysis.
  3. Conversation analysis. 4. Communication in education.
  I. Title. II. Series
  P95.535.T7 1996
    302.2–dc20   96-43667
                                            CIP

Ablex Publishing Corporation
355 Chestnut Street
Norwood, New Jersey 07648

This book is dedicated to Herb Simons, whose fondness for talking about ideas, and passion in so doing, inspired this project.

Contents

Preface to the Series

ROY O. FREEDLE
SERIES EDITOR

This series of volumes provides a forum for the cross-fertilization of ideas from a diverse number of disciplines, all of which share a common interest in discourse—be it prose comprehension and recall, dialogue analysis, text grammar construction, computer simulation of natural language, cross cultural comparisons of communicative competence or other related topics. The problems posed by multisentence contexts and the methods required to investigate them, while not always unique to discourse, are still sufficiently distinct as to benefit from the organized model of scientific interaction made possible by this series.

Scholars working in the discourse area from the perspective of sociolinguistics, psycholinguistics, ethnomethodology and the sociology of language, educational psychology (e.g., teacher–student interaction), the philosophy of language, computational linguistics, and related subareas are invited to submit manuscripts of monograph or book length to the series editor. Edited collections of original papers resulting from conferences will also be considered.

VOLUMES IN THE SERIES

Acknowledgments

Many people contributed to this book, helping cultivate what was initially but an obsessive curiosity and an insight or two. To each of them I extend my heartfelt thanks. First and foremost are the colleagues and students who talked with me about academic discussion and allowed me to record them doing it. As I worked through how best to frame the book's central claims, Sheryl Baratz, John Bowers, Kristine Fitch, Barry Liss, Julie Naughton, and Herb Simons were especially helpful. Each acted as a sounding board and/or gave thoughtful and extensive comments on drafts of the manuscript. Bob Craig merits special mention. Besides providing extensive, frequent, and helpful feedback, he provided encouragement when I needed it and helped me see humor in the contradictory fears about which I worried (Will these claims be judged trivial and obvious? Will these claims be seen as outrageous and completely unpersuasive?). Finally thanks to my daughter, Jill Tracy-Craig, who helped me stay happy and not get too obsessive.

Segments of the book have been reworked from papers that initially appeared as journal articles and conference proceedings. A good part of chapter 2 appeared in "Intellectual discussion in the academy as situated discourse," *Communication Monographs, 60* (1993), coauthored with Sheryl Baratz. Segments of chapter 3 and chapter 7 appeared in "Identity enactment in intellectual discussion," in the *Journal of Language and Social Psychology, 12* (1993), coauthored with Jioanna Carjuzaa. Much of the analysis in chapter 4 appeared in the article "The identity work of questioning in intellectual discussion," that was published in *Communication Monographs, 61* (1994), and was coauthored with Julie Naughton. Segments of chapters 6 and 8 appeared in "Talking about ideas: Academics' beliefs about appropriate communicative practices" in *Research on Language and Social Interaction, 27* (1994), coathored with Nicole Muller. The discussion of situated ideals in chapter 10 initially appeared in "Grounded practical theory: The case of intellectual discussion" in *Communication Theory,* (1995), coauthored with Robert Craig. Chapter 10 was presented at the Ninth SCA/AFA Conference on Argumentation and appeared in the conference proceedings (Tracy,1995b).

1

Colloquium: an Introduction

It's 2:30 Monday afternoon in the State U communication department. In one corner of Room 207, the graduate student teachers' office, Steve is explaining a paper assignment to an anxious-looking student; in another, Marianne is highlighting a book she is reading. Linda, Bill, and Susan are joking about faculty foibles while they discuss advantages and problems involved in working with each. Rachel enters the office, deposits a stack of books on an already cluttered desk, looks at the clock, and announces to all present, "It's time."

In Room 212, Alice Twellen logs out of an electronic mail program, shuts off her computer, grabs pen and paper, and leaves the office. Ed Jones, inhabitant of Office 213, interrupts Randy Elgin's comments about his proposed seminar paper to say "It's time to go upstairs." Reid Hastings, Jones's office neighbor, marks the journal article he is reading, picks up his coffee cup, and heads down the hallway. Hastings stops at Room 215 to ask Tim Rasnow if he is ready. Tim smiles, makes a joke, and says he'll be right up.

In his office, Tim looks through the notes he has been reviewing, pencils in a final phrase—Reid is sure to go after *that* claim—and puts the pages in order. He spends a moment regretting that he hadn't made himself get up a half hour earlier. I don't want to blow it the way Ed did, he thinks. After performing a final check on his notes, he heads toward the upstairs' seminar room, Room 322, mentally rehearsing his opening comments. He detours to visit the bathroom and water fountain.[1]

---

1. In a review article, Bowers, Metts, and Duncanson (1985) identify frequent urination and a tight throat as two behaviors that signal strong emotional arousal.

As Tim enters the seminar room, Susan laughingly asks him if he's ready for the hot seat.

In Room 322, first arrivals take seats at the long rectangular table dominating the room. Two first-semester graduate students glance at the table as they enter, but choose chairs distant from the table. Bill, a second-year student, selects a chair at the table as he reminds himself that he has to ask at least one question; no more sitting there like a lump. Rachel, a student working on her dissertation, sits next to Bill and jokes that it'll be her turn for the guillotine next week. As she gazes around the room she thinks how great it would be if she could say something insightful in the discussion period. I'm going to ask a challenging question, she thinks, one that opens up issues in an interesting way. Well, pretty challenging; I don't want Tim out to get me in my dissertation.

Others arrive. Greetings, friendly banter, and appointment-making occur. A tall gray-haired man enters and moves a chair from its place against the wall to the table. People at the table squeeze closer. Faculty member Alice announces that Jeff sends his regrets about not being there because he had to attend a college committee meeting.

At 2:45, the seminar room has eight faculty members and 11 graduate students. Tim Rasnow is sitting at the head of the table, Andrew Elkins immediately to his right. Andrew gets the group's attention and introduces Tim and the title of his talk. Tim looks around the group, pulls his notes forward, and begins: "In conclusion, I think . . . " Laughter erupts from the group. Tim joins in the laughter and then says, "Okay, okay; I think I'm ready now." Tim starts his presentation, adding comments to his pre-planned notes as he notices people shaking their heads as if in disagreement, or puzzlement. Forty minutes later he concludes.

Discussion begins. Reid, Alice, Ed, Ron, Rachel, Bill, and others question Tim, challenge his assertions, query his assumptions. After 35 minutes of sometimes heated, sometimes boring, and occasionally funny exchanges, Andrew admonishes, "Last question. It's four o'clock." Tim answers the question. The group applauds. People leave the seminar room, chatting as they go.

Leaving the colloquium, Bill pats himself on the back for asking a question. It wasn't a tough one, he reflects, but at least I opened my mouth.

Ron, a senior professor, silently argues with himself about the reasonableness of his actions. Bad ideas need to be recognized for what they are, he thinks. He couldn't let that kind of intellectual sloppiness pass; he had to say something. Still, he feels bad that he pushed so hard. Tim was overly defensive and didn't handle it well. Ron imagines a future conversation with Reid in which Reid accuses him of being a show-off.

Alice, too, is reflecting about her own behavior: Why did I drop my issue so quickly? I should have pushed it harder. Tim's a big boy. I'm being too much of a Milquetoast. People are going to think I'm not very smart. I can't or won't speak out. Why am I censoring my disagreement? This is an intellectual discussion, not a therapy session.

Watching people leave the room, Tim begins to relax. People seemed interested in what I was saying, he thinks, it went Okay. I wish that I had made my point a little more clearly. I shouldn't have let Ron get to me but Ron does that.

Andrew leaves the seminar room with Tim. "Enjoyed it," he says, "but where were all the graduate students? And why are they so quiet? Other than Rachel and Mike, nobody said much."

State U's weekly colloquium is over.

By participating in this colloquium, State U faculty and graduate students have enacted the university's most privileged and noble mission: the advancing and testing of ideas, the production of truth and knowledge, a communicative activity that is the "the essential sound for a place of thought" (Billig, 1986, p. 21).[2] As ideas advance and are tested, though, what are people doing? What is the role for emotions and relationships? What worries do faculty and graduate students bring to this occasion? What problems do participants face as they talk with each other? How are problems made visible in talk and given attention through talk?

Intellectual dialogue is something about which philosophers have written extensively (e.g., Gadamer, 1984; Habermas, 1979; Rorty, 1989). With only a few exceptions, however, intellectual discussion as an occasion of talk has not been studied.[3] Given the importance of intellectual discussion in universities, and the diversity of other institutional talk practices that have been examined, this lack of attention is curious.[4] In this book I describe, interpret, and critique academics doing intellectual discussion.

[2.] In her book *Talking Power,* Robin Lakoff (1990) wryly comments: "In this semantic of noble purpose, we can define the university's mission as the production of truth or knowledge, a virtuous enterprise if there ever was one" (p. 144).

[3.] Grimshaw (1989, 1994) studies a segment from a dissertation defense and Potter (1984; McKinlay & Potter, 1987) examines segments of psychologists' discussions at an academic conference.

[4.] That is, recent scholarship has provided us a sense of what talk looks like in jury deliberations (Manzo, 1993), plea bargaining (Maynard, 1984), the courtroom (Aronsson, 1991; Conley & O'Barr, 1990; Penman, 1987; Penman; 1991; Woodbury, 1984), decision-making meetings in schools and universities (Bailey, 1983; Mehan, 1986), interviews with government officials (Boynton, 1991; Orr, 1980; Walton, 1989), police interrogations (Linell & Jonsson, 1991), divorce mediation (Tracy & Spradlin, 1994), counseling and therapy (Buttny, 1990; Buttny & Cohen, 1991, Labov & Fanshel, 1977), between doctors and patients (Aronsson & Rundstrom, 1989; Fisher & Todd, 1986, Tannen & Wallet, 1993), dentists and patients (Anderson, 1986), nurse-practitioners and patients (Ragan, 1990), health care teams (Sands, 1993; Soyland, 1994), classrooms (Heath, 1983; Michaels & Collins, 1984), scientific laboratories (Knorr-Cetina, 1981; Latour & Woolgar, 1986, Lynch, 1985), radio and television broadcasts (Carbaugh, 1988; Gaik, 1992; Kuo, 1994) and so on. We know little about intellectual discussion in the academy, however.

My central purpose is to understand better this institutionally significant activity. In doing so, I focus on one particular type of intellectual discussion—the departmental colloquium. Drawing upon tape-recorded colloquia, interviews with colloquium participants, and several other kinds of materials, I describe the web of problems academic groups face, the discursive practices used, and the ideals academics have about how they should talk. I focus on the departmental colloquium for two reasons.

First, the departmental colloquium is the most frequent site where academics "do" intellectual discussion and, as graduate students, learn how it is done. As an academic, I care about ideas and like to talk about them with others. Yet too often the discussions in which I participate have problems, and everyone leaves feeling dissatisfied. I want to understand better why this happens. What is going on, and what is going wrong? Are there ways to improve academic discussions? Is it a matter of how we frame the activity? Its routine structures? Who gets to participate? What is said, and what remains unsaid? Thus, I study the academic colloquium because it is a forum about which I care deeply, and because of its importance in university life. I seek to understand how colloquium works in order to contribute ideas that could improve its practice.

Second, study of the departmental colloquium provides an especially interesting arena in which to examine a basic communicative process: the enactment, challenging, and altercasting of identity. Colloquium is, as one interviewee remarked, "a good thing to study because things happen there that are curious and of interest . . . it's a good place where egos are on the line . . . and how people present themselves matters really." It is the appropriate management of self, the inevitability of one's talk implying a view of the other, the difficulties inherent in seeking to enact contradictory valued qualities, that are the central interactional problems colloquium participants face. To understand better how talk enacts identities, it is necessary to look at people talking in situations in which it is consequential for them. The departmental colloquium is that kind of occasion.

COLLOQUIUM AS A DILEMMATIC SITUATION

The central claim I develop in this book is that the academic colloquium is best conceived as a dilemmatic situation—a communicative occasion involving tensions and contradiction. This claim has three layers of meaning. The first layer concerns the character of problems that participants face. Through analyses of academics' talk about the occasion, colloquium problems are shown to involve multiple dilemmas. A second meaning layer involves how a dilemmatic frame can shape understanding of conversational action. Against a dilemmatic backdrop, mundane, supposedly trivial conversational actions in colloquium become recognizable as strategic moves to accomplish interpersonal and group goals. The final layer has to do with suitable situational ideals. Having analyzed the problems and conversational practices, I consider how academics ought to conduct themselves in colloquium. Toward that end, I advance three principles, all of which, albeit in slightly different ways, draw upon a dilemmatic logic. Thus, the value of a dilemmatic perspective for understanding colloquium is displayed by showing how (a) colloquium problems that academics experience as diffuse and hard to articulate become recognizable, (b) an array of conversational minutiae becomes sensible, and (c) specific moral/practical proposals emerge as defensible and desirable courses of action.

Dilemmatic perspectives, while not dominant approaches to inquiry, have informed scholarly problem analyses in diverse domains, and are visible as far back as Aristotle. In the *Nichomachean Ethics* Aristotle described virtuous action as lying in a middle ground between contrary impulses such that, for example, being courageous requires a person to resist impulses toward cowardice and impulses toward foolhardiness.[5]

Explanations of the problems that leaders in social movements must confront (Simons, 1970), the difficulties scientists face in doing good work (Kaplan, 1964; Pelz & Andrews, 1976), and the problems friends and spouses encounter in close relationships have all drawn upon dilemmatic perspectives. Recent work on close relationships, for instance, has shifted from conceiving of relational problems as difficulties in achieving single goals such as getting close to another, or reducing uncertainty about how to act, to conceiving of relational problems as fundamentally requiring each party to "manage" incompatible wants: desires for autonomy and connection, relational stability and novelty, self-expressiveness and an expectation that one will protect the other (Baxter, 1988; Rawlins, 1989, 1991; Tannen, 1984).[6] In addition, tensions have been identified in a myriad of routine talk occasions. In making requests, giving feedback on a work task, or talking with another of a different age, gender or ethnicity, communicators have been portrayed as possessing multiple (and often contrary) interactional goals and interpersonal concerns (Tracy, 1984, 1991).

Perhaps most relevant to this study of the academic colloquium is Michael Billig's analysis of everyday thinking (Billig, 1987; Billig et al., 1988). Billig characterizes everyday thinking as dilemmatic. By this he means that people's ordinary reflections about what they believe and what they think is appropriate can be expected to contain contrary themes.

[5.] See Aristotle (1941, pp. 959–960).

[6.] Werner and Baxter (1994) and Baxter and Montgomery (1996) provide reviews of the different dilemmatic approaches with an emphasis on their character in close relationships.

These contrary themes are essential to productive thought. Thinking requires tension; without it, there is no motivating force for reflection.

What it means to conceive of colloquium as dilemmatic will become clearer as the analysis proceeds. Two comments at this point: First, although all the problems to be unveiled involve tensions among beliefs, not all involve direct contradiction. In that sense, my use of the term *dilemma* draws most consistently upon the concept's weaker meaning (tensions) than upon its stronger meaning (absolute contradiction).[7] Second, in exploring dilemmas of colloquium, I treat dilemmas as positioned. That is, I assume that the character of a dilemma will be shaped by whose view of the situation we take. Problems that confront individuals in their roles as presenters will differ from the problems that confront discussants, which in turn will differ from those faced by the group as a whole.

INTELLECTUAL DISCUSSION: A LOOSE-FITTING FRAME

I described the academic colloquium as a kind of intellectual discussion. In characterizing the colloquium as intellectual discussion, I am invoking the notion of situational frame. Bateson (1972) defines a situational frame as a set of expectations about the nature of an occasion, the social meaning of a unit of interaction.[8] On the basis of the interviews described below, several expectations inform the intellectual discussion frame.[9]

Most basically, intellectual discussion is a talk occasion in which the primary focus is on ideas. Furthermore, the ideas are ones of some abstraction—not, in the words of one faculty member, "how to plant your beans." In addition, participants are expected to explore differences of opinion when, at least in principle, they are open to changing their minds as a result of talking. Finally, the occasion is valued as an end in and of itself, not simply as a tool to be used to accomplish other ends such as making a decision, or teaching information to another. This does not mean that intellectual discussants do not learn, or that what is said has no implications for subsequent decision-making, but it does mean that these purposes are secondary foci in the occasion. Intellectual discussion is not the

---

[7.] It is not easy to determine when situational tensions are contradictory. Often what is absolutely incompatible in one context becomes only a "tension" in another. Whether two beliefs are contradictory will depend on the nature of the interactional context. For instance, treating people as equals and recognizing status/authority differences are contradictory injunctions only in situations in which participants are of different status levels.

[8.] The definition of *frame* upon which I draw is not its only meaning. Tannen (1993) reviews how different disciplinary traditions have used the concept.

[9.] These definitional criteria were derived from interviews with faculty and graduate students at University X, described below.

only frame that could be applied to the academic colloquium, but using intellectual discussion as the dominant frame, rather than, say, "doing science" or engaging in "professional talk,"[10] can provide valuable new insights. Understanding the problems of colloquium, its discursive practices, and academics' beliefs about how they ought to act is facilitated by the intellectual discussion frame. In the remainder of this chapter, I describe the intellectual discussion materials on which the book is based, say more about two theoretical issues, describe the discourse analytic method used, and present an overview of the book.

CENTRAL CASE: STATE U'S COLLOQUIUM

The analysis to be presented is based on several kinds of data collected from a variety of settings and institutions. The primary data come from "State U," a state-affiliated research university in the United States. Starting in 1988 and extending over a two-year period, weekly colloquia in a Ph.D.-granting communication department were audiotaped, field notes taken, and interviews conducted. Participants were faculty and graduate students in the department with occasional visitors from other departments and universities.

Communication as an academic field is less well defined than are some of the longer-established disciplines. In colleges and universities around the United States, it is typically either one of a set of departments in a College of Communication or a department in a College of Arts and Sciences. Departments go by a variety of names, with the most common being communication arts, communication studies, speech, or speech communication. Some communication departments include mass media studies; others are separated from departments or schools of mass media. Debates are common about whether communication is a discipline or an interdisciplinary area of study. Newsletters of the major professional organizations, as well as occasional special issues of a journal, carry opinion pieces about the field's character and intellectual center.[11] In addition, communication does not fall neatly into the academic categories of social scientific or humanistic study. Instead, individual scholars align with one,

---

[10] Grimshaw (1989, 1994) labeled the talk that occurred in a dissertation defense as professional talk; Potter (1984) labeled the discussion of psychologists at academic conferences as "science" talk. The significance of situational frames is discussed in chapter 11.

[11] Examples of this are regularly seen in the monthly newsletter of the Speech Communication Association, *Spectra*. In 1983 the *Journal of Communication* published a special issue, which included 35 essays and was titled "Ferment in the Field." More recently this same journal had a 10-year retrospective resulting in two quarterly issues devoted to the topic, which was simultaneously released as a book (Levy & Gurevitch, 1994).

the other, or both of these orientations based on their training and/or inclinations.

At State U, roughly half of the faculty aligned with humanistic study, and more particularly contemporary rhetorical studies. The other half defined themselves as social scientists, with interests in a range of face-to-face communicative settings. The intellectual thread that bound this group together (and arguably distinguishes communication as a field) was an interest in messages, with a concurrent assumption that messages are designed for particular audiences and situations.

At the time that my formal observation began, the colloquium was in its fifth year of existence. Prior to that time there had been sporadic colloquia that occurred several times a semester. These colloquia were sometimes well attended, but often not. Attendance in prior years had been strongly influenced by a presenter's standing in the departmental and disciplinary community. In 1984–85 the department began to hold a colloquium every Monday afternoon during the academic year.

A significant reason for creating the weekly colloquium at State U was to combat the sense of intellectual isolation that was prevalent in this urban university. Evidence that State U's colloquium was designed to be responsive to this concern is seen in a written document prepared by the department as part of a routine graduate program evaluation around the time of this study. The departmental self-study described the purpose of colloquium this way:

> In addition to the information/learning value of the colloquium, it is per-
> haps the major vehicle we have to express ongoing friendly relations with
> each other and sustain our sense of intellectual community. The colloquia
> provide a relatively supportive public forum in which students and faculty
> can develop the ability to present ideas to a critical audience.

The colloquium at State U was held in the same room every week, a room housing a rectangular table that seated about 15, with room for another 15 people in a second tier of chairs against the walls. Attendance was voluntary and varied from 10 to 25 participants, with average attendance hovering around 20. Regular attenders included eight to nine faculty, two of whom were women, with students making up the remaining participants. Among the students there were roughly twice as many women as men.[12] The typical colloquium format included a thirty to fifty-minute presentation followed by a twenty-five to forty-five-minute discussion.

[12.] In the graduate program there were roughly twice as many female students as males. My perception was that colloquium attendance reflected this ratio, however, individual attendance was not recorded.

Often the actual start of a presentation was preceded by a series of brief announcements. State U participants were reminded about upcoming conference deadlines, volunteers were sought to help with some aspect of work involved in a yearly conference, people were informed about departmental social occasions, and so on.

Work presented in the colloquium varied from papers in the beginning stages to already published work. Topics included, for example, an analysis of presidential campaign strategies, an analysis of how managers motivate in the workplace, conceptions of intercultural communication, and issues in religious broadcasting. Doctoral students were required to make one presentation at the colloquium. Of these colloquia, full discussion periods from 10 occasions, as well as selected excerpts from others, have been transcribed.[13]

To provide a sense of participants' beliefs about the nature of the colloquium situation and its interactional problems, interviews were conducted with 10 regularly attending participants—six faculty members and four graduate students. The interviews consisted of 20 open-ended questions and lasted about 35 minutes. Questions were designed to explore participants' understandings of group and individual-level goals for colloquium. Appendix A includes the interview schedule and more extensive information about interviewees and procedures.

I was a faculty member in the department in which the State U colloquium occurred. The colloquium tapings and interviews occurred soon after my tenuring and promotion to associate professor. The role of a researcher in relation to the people he or she studies has elicited considerable thought and debate in recent years. This concern has been most pronounced in ethnographic study but is also present in discourse analytic studies. Two questions have dominated the scholarly discussion:

1. What are the advantages and disadvantages of studying the cultural "other" rather than groups of which one is a member (see Adler & Adler, 1987)?

2. Is the goal of analysis to be descriptive or critical (e.g., Fiske, 1991; Philipsen, 1991; van Dijk, 1993)?

---

13. Discussions selected for transcription reflect all possible configurations of given identities—faculty and students in the department, and faculty and students outside the department. Within that broad constraint, selection of discussions was influenced by: (a) audiotape quality: Depending on the placement of the recorder and which participants were most talkative, tapes varied in their audibility. More audible tapes were selected. (b) perceived level of discussion involvement: Based on participation-observation, discussions where more participants seemed involved were selected over those where fewer participants seemed involved; and (c) my knowledge about a presentation topic.

In writing this book, I meld description with criticism, and bring the advantages (and potential disadvantages) of being an insider. That is, this analysis is shaped by my investment in academe as an institution, my commitment to communication as a field of academic study, and my professional and emotional involvement with the colleagues and students whose discussions and interviews I study. I mark my role and commitments in this situation to make clear to readers the position from which interpretations are offered.

SECONDARY MATERIALS

In addition to the State U case, several other kinds of materials are used in a supplemental way. The most extensive secondary materials are interviews collected from "University X," a major state university in a different geographic region of the United States. Chapters 6 and 8 draw heavily on these interviews. Participants for this second set of interviews were 20 faculty and Ph.D. students in a communication department at that university. Like State U, the department held a weekly colloquium. In contrast to State U's research paper focus, the typical format at University X involved open-ended discussion of articles or a book suggested by one of the participants. Attendance at University X's colloquium was voluntary for faculty but was part of a course requirement for graduate students.

At University X, I interviewed regularly attending participants after one year in which I was a participant-observer.[14] Interviewees were selected on the basis of colloquium attendance. Faculty and graduate students who attended colloquium three or more times over the year were interviewed. Interviewees included 13 faculty and 7 graduate students. Participants were asked to describe and reflect upon their experiences in the departmental colloquium specifically, and their experiences with intellectual discussion more broadly. Specific issues included characteristics of the departmental colloquium that participants liked or disliked, self-presentation concerns, definitions of intellectual discussion, and distinguishing

---

[14.] The pattern of attendance at University X's colloquia was different from State U's. Students at University X were required to take colloquium as course credit and attend for a year. With rare exceptions, only those graduate students taking the colloquium for credit attended. Among the faculty, attendance was good among tenured faculty—full and associate professors—but considerably poorer among assistant professors. An upshot of this attendance pattern was that a typical colloquium involved the most senior faculty and the most junior graduate students. Senior graduate students and junior faculty were notably absent.

good discussions from poor ones. In all, 26 open-ended questions were asked. The interview schedule and more details about the interviewees and procedures are included in Appendix B.

While the departmental colloquium is the focal kind of intellectual discussion examined, it is not the only kind. Analyses draw upon other kinds of discussions, including a seminar at an academic professional meeting, an interdepartmental faculty symposium, and the opening exchanges of a dissertation defense. Appendix C provides an overview of these materials.

GROUNDED PRACTICAL THEORY: THE APPROACH TO INQUIRY

The theoretical perspective that has informed this project is Robert Craig's (1989, 1992, 1993, Craig & Tracy, 1995) work on communication as a practical discipline. In the perspective of communication as a practical discipline,

> [i]nquiry moves in a hermeneutic circle of preinterpretation, action, critical reflection, reinterpretation, and further action. "Theory" (conceptual thought) and "practice" (situated action) can be understood as moments within this process; and a practical discipline can be defined as a formal scholarly enterprise that attempts to extend, facilitate, and inform this reflective cycle of thought and action by engaging in systematic, critical study and theoretical reconstruction of practices in society. "Theoretical reconstruction" of a practice means that the practice is typified or *idealized* such that particular instances are redescribed in less context-specific, more universalized terms. In idealizing a practice, a theoretical reconstruction also *rationalizes* it so that values and principles implicit in the practice are made explicit and a reasoned basis for "good practice" and critical judgments of practice is constructed. Practical theory can thus be thought of as a *rational reconstruction* of practice. (Craig & Tracy, 1995, p. 252)

Using this project as a case, the practical discipline conception has been elaborated into a more explicit metatheoretical frame—grounded practical theory (Craig & Tracy, 1995).

In grounded practical theory, communicative practices are reconstructed at three interrelated levels. The first and most central is the problem level, where the web of problems or dilemmas that confront practitioners as they participate in a communicative situation are articulated. At the second level of reconstruction, the technical level, the conversational moves and discursive techniques used to manage problems are described. At the third, the philosophical level, the normative ideals that furnish the rationale for resolving problems are reconstructed.[15]

In this book, problems of the academic colloquium are examined from two perspectives: that of the colloquium group, and that of individual participants in their roles as discussants and presenters. In viewing problems from the individual's vantage point, key dilemmas are seen to revolve around conflicting identity wants.

IDENTITY AND IDENTITY-WORK

The notion that a person's identity is negotiated through communication is by no means new. Initially proposed by symbolic interactionists (e.g., Mead, 1934), the idea has recently taken on new life in the broad-based intellectual movement known as social constructionism (e.g., Harre, 1987; Shotter, 1993). Central to both symbolic interactionist thought and social constructionism is the notion that selves are constructed, maintained, and challenged by communicative practices. In this book, I extend this general insight to show how, in academic colloquia, identity construction works at the level of conversational specifics. I show that very particular discourse devices serve as the bricks and mortar with which academics build identities as they cope with the interactional dilemmas they face.

In writing about persons and communicative practices, scholars have used three sets of similar terms: (a) self and self-presentation (e.g., Baumeister, 1986; Tedeschi, 1990); (b) face and facework (e.g., Brown & Levinson, 1987; Goffman, 1955); and (c) identity and identity work[16] (e.g., Shotter & Gergen, 1989). While these terms overlap considerably in meaning, and all three sets appear in this book, *identity* is the dominant concept. I privilege *identity* and *identity-work* over the other concepts because these terms avoid several associations I find troublesome.

In particular, the concept *self* aligns personhood with stable internal feelings, thoughts, and intentions (Geertz, 1984; Potter & Wetherell, 1987). In contrast, *identity* gives greater weight to the interactive social world as the location of personhood. Identity is who one is and how one

---

[15.] In contrast to other normative theories that presuppose a philosophically-derived ideal for the critique of practice—e.g., the pragma-dialectical theory of critical discussion (van Eemeren & Grootendorst, 1984; Van Eemeren, Grootendorst, Jackson, & Jacobs, 1993)—grounded practical theory reconstructs ideals by articulating the inchoate normative principles, that is the "situated ideals," that participants actually use to reflect upon and criticize action. Because technical and philosophical thinking are expected to enter reflection only as they become relevant to problems, the problem level is the pivotal one.

[16.] *Identity* is a term gaining widespread use in the social sciences and humanities among scholars taking a social constructionist viewpoint. My term "identity-work" flips the focus from the situated self to the communicative actions of discourse.

acts in a given situation (Fitzgerald, 1993). Moreover, much more than the term *self presentation, identity* (and *identity-work*) recognizes that communication is implicative for all participants. Not only does communication involve presenting self, but it involves altercasting, implying one's view of the other. To use identity as the theoretical lens is to promote the awareness that conversational moves are always other- as well as self-implicative.

Second, while both *face* and *identity* implicitly reject an internalized, decontexualized view of self, the concept *face* does so in a way that does not entirely escape a sense of cynicism and superficiality. Initially developed by Erving Goffman (1955, 1959) in his dramaturgical view of social interaction, *face*, like identity, draws attention to personhood as a situated enactment rather than a stable way of being (self). Yet, as its everyday use suggests ("It's *just* a matter of face; she needs to get past that"), *face*, nonetheless, supports a view of the world that distinguishes image from substance, the appearance of things from reality. In this dichotomy, face cannot escape being the superficial part of the pair. In contrast the term *identity* highlights how being and appearing are indistinguishable parts of the same process: Who one is can be known only through how one comes across in particular occasions. Put another way, the terms *identity* and *identity-work* better capture a view of the social construction of persons as morally serious business.

Finally, the concept *identity* frees inquiry from the inappropriately high level of abstraction implied by the most widely used conception of face— that of Brown and Levinson (1987), who define *positive face* as the desire to be appreciated and approved of by selected others, and *negative face* as the desire to be free from impingement from others. While Brown and Levinson recognize cultural variations in how these wants are expressed, the concerns are formulated as universal ones that are relevant to all people in all situations.

Brown and Levinson's face conceptions are not unreasonable characterizations of people's situational concerns, and these conceptions have been used as the theoretical lens to make sense of a large number of diverse speech occasions.[17] Nonetheless, they are less than optimally helpful. People's situated identity concerns are more particular than positive and negative face; that is, when a person gives a formal presentation to a

---

17. Politeness theory has been used as the analytic frame for written texts and verbal interaction as diverse as doctor-patient exchanges (Aronsson & Rundstrom, 1989), tenure appeal letters in universities (Wood & Kroger, 1994), journal articles (Myers, 1989), Shakespeare's plays (Brown & Gilman, 1989), courtroom interaction (Penman, 1990), problems in aviation discourse (Linde, 1988), negotiation processes (Wilson, 1992) and broad-based interpersonal message processes (Craig, Tracy, & Spisak, 1986; Lim & Bowers, 1991). Although most analyses have focused on English speakers, politeness theory has informed conversational analyses in other languages including Polish (Jaworski, 1994), Swahili (Yahya-Othman, 1994), and Greek (Pavlidou, 1991; Sifianou, 1989). Reviews and critiques of politeness theory are numerous and include Fraser (1990), Ting-Toomey (1994), Tracy (1990) and Wood and Kroger (1994) to identify but a few of the more recently published ones.

group, participates in a decision-making meeting at work, deals with the misbehavior of a child, or chats at a party, the identity that the person seeks to uphold for self, as well as altercast for others, is going to be different. Although these goals can be glossed as a person's concerns for self and other's face, such a gloss leaves unelaborated what is most interesting: the situation-specific wants and conversational strategies. Thus, a final reason for preferring the concept identity is to encourage analysis at a specificity level compatible with the way people experience those wants.

ACTION-IMPLICATIVE DISCOURSE ANALYSIS

Action-implicative discourse analysis, the methodological reasoning procedure used in this project, is a method used to reconstruct the problems and situated ideals actors have, and the conversational techniques used to address problems. As with other types of discourse analysis, a first step involves tape recording talk in the social situation of interest, followed by preparation of written transcripts. The decision concerning which interactional specifics to preserve in the transcription system is a key feature distinguishing among different discourse analytic approaches, but common to all types of discourse analysis is a commitment to reproduce what was said in the manner in which it was spoken. This means that group discussions and interviews are not cleaned up to rid them of repetitions, repairs, word and sentence fragments, vocalized pauses, and so on, that are part of ordinary speech. Appendix D explains the transcription symbols used in this book.

For readers unaccustomed to reading written transcripts of natural speech, a first reaction is to presume that the people represented in a transcript must be extremely inarticulate, perhaps even of limited intelligence. This is a reasonable first reaction, since novels and plays—the forms in which most people are exposed to written speech—seldom represent speech in its naturally occurring style. Not only do literary forms represent conversation differently; so too do public records of political hearings, organizational meetings, and courtroom trials. In the courtroom, for instance, transcripts are routinely cleaned up to insure that the speech of at least the primary players (judges, attorneys, expert witnesses) sounds "educated" (Walker, 1986).

The reason discourse analysts seek to create a precise record of a talk exchange is that these conversational specifics—a chopped-off phrase, replacement of one pronoun with another (e.g., *We* for *I*), specifying the exact place where nonfluent speech occurs (e.g., *uh, uhm*), and so on—are taken to be resources to do conversational work, not just errors or verbal garbage. Besides the commitment to recording and transcribing speech, a second feature of discourse analytic work is its usage of instances of transcribed speech, along with analytic commentary, as a central means through which to formulate scholarly arguments.

While action-implicative discourse analysis shares these points of commonality with other discourse approaches, it is distinctive in several ways.[18] First, as previously mentioned, it takes as its central purpose the reconstruction of communicator problems, conversational techniques to address problems, and participants' situated ideals. This focus on what is problematic for communicators contrasts with the approach that has come to be labeled conversation analysis (Atkinson & Heritage, 1984; Schegloff, 1992) in which the goal is to explain how social action is organized through conversational particulars.

Second, as a discourse analytic method whose goal is to understand communicative problems, it routinely seeks to uncover what participants may be inferring about each other. Thus, also in contrast to conversation analysis (Schegloff, 1992), action-implicative discourse analysis uses informational sources that go beyond those made available through talk. In particular, action-implicative discourse analysis draws upon a researcher's knowledge gained through participation in a community, as well as interviews with participants, to make visible the community's likely interpretive practices; that is, action-implicative discourse analysis uses ethnographic background information to inform discourse interpretations.[19]

Third and relatedly, action-implicative discourse analysis is interested in both the discourse of an occasion (the interaction) and the discourse about an occasion (interviews). In contrast to many kinds of ethnographic work, however, interviews are treated as a form of discourse (Coupland, Coupland, Giles, & Henwood, 1991; Mishler, 1986; Potter & Wetherell, 1987). Treating interviews as discourse has two implications. It presumes that interviews, like other kinds of speech, are rhetorical in form, designed for the particular other and the occasion, a feature that is essential to keep in mind in interpreting an interview. In addition, since interviews are conceived as discursive events, they are transcribed in an identical fashion to the interactive discourse. Thus, just as nonfluencies, repetitions, verbal

---

18. Discourse analytic approaches differ in transcription practices, the role of context, central theoretical questions, and metatheoretical perspectives. Elsewhere (Tracy, 1995b) I describe action-implicative discourse analysis and contrast it with conversation analysis (e.g., Atkinson & Heritage, 1984), interactional sociolinguistics (e.g., Gumperz, 1982a, 1982b), critical discourse analysis (e.g., Fairclough, 1992; Hodge & Kress, 1993) and discursive psychology (Edwards & Potter, 1992; Potter & Wetherell, 1987).

19. Whether this type of contextual information should be used to interpret talk, is a matter on which discourse analysts strongly disagree (Duranti & Goodwin, 1992). On this issue, my position is similar to Cicourel's (1992).

fillers, and false starts are included in transcripts of interactive speech situations, so too are they included in interview transcripts.

Although both interviews and interaction are discourse, they are understood somewhat differently. Interview discourse is conceived of as a metadiscourse about an interactive occasion. In this project, then, interview discourse is analyzed to capture the interactional problems and situated ideals of the academic colloquium. In attempting to characterize problems and ideals, people's answers to interview questions are not necessarily taken as straightforward descriptions of "the way things are." Rather, direct answers are interpreted in light of implicit evaluations conveyed in comments. For instance, although two people might both say that a central purpose of intellectual discussion is to critique ideas (explicit answer), if Person A contrasts a current focal occasion with past experiences by describing *past* experiences as "incredibly lively and exciting" and Person B contrasts the same current focal occasion with past experiences by remarking how the *current* situation has much less "barracuda talk," we have evidence that the two have different beliefs about how critique should be conducted. A's remark implies that discussion situations should have the qualities of liveliness and excitement; B implies that appropriate idea critique involves avoiding aggressive, people-destroying talk. Moreover, A's and B's remarks imply a different assessment of how well the current group is conducting itself. In praising the group for not succumbing to a common problem (barracuda talk), rather than criticizing it for what it lacks (no liveliness), B implies a much more positive assessment of group practices than does A. Thus, action-implicative discourse analysis uses evaluations conveyed in reflections about experiences and practices to infer what implicit beliefs (or problems) people must hold. It is in situation-engendered reflections that people reveal a facet of what they believe, but would not (or could not) articulate explicitly.

A fourth distinctive feature of action-implicative discourse analysis is its analytic goal with regard to interactive discourse. Action-implicative discourse analysis seeks to describe conversational moves to address communicative problems.[20] Just as Brown and Levinson (1987) show how a whole set of conversational devices can be seen as politeness strategies, this analytic method seeks to show how certain conversational moves are interpretable as interactional strategies that are responding to participants' identity, or group-level, dilemmas. Stated somewhat differently, action-implicative discourse analysis is not primarily making claims about what

---

[20] Any specific conversational action could have meanings (outcomes) very different from the ones described. For instance if participants possessed a certain relational history, if the vocal intonation were atypical, if unusual facial expressions were present—any of these features could change the situated meaning of the conversational move. Since this kind of analysis does not attend to all aspects of conversational action or every kind of contextual feature I cannot, and do not, claim to capture what actually happened.

actually happened—what speakers in particular instances intended, or what recipients inferred. Instead, through close analysis of discourse instances, it seeks to describe potential likely meanings for conversational actions in the situation of interest. In sum, determining what is the clearest and most helpful way to characterize communicative problems, conversational strategies and situated ideals—the end goal of action-implicative discourse analysis—is accomplished by shifting analytic focus back and forth between interactive and interview discourse.

OVERVIEW OF THE BOOK

In the first section of the book, chapters 2 through 5, the academic colloquium is viewed from the vantage point of individual participants, considering both what dilemmas are faced, and what conversational strategies are used. Chapter 2 lays out the beliefs the State U group brought to their weekly colloquium. As graduate students and faculty members in their roles as presenters and discussants, participants confronted problems. Whatever course of action State U academics selected, they risked being seen in an undesirable light. Chapter 2 describes these dilemmas.

Chapter 3 examines how academics frame their work at the start of formal presentations, and how participants account for actions. I show how specific lexical formulations enact presenters as intimate with, or distant from, the ideas about which they talk. This positioning of self, I suggest, is interpretable as the individual's situated resolution to the problems raised by institutional rank and topical expertise. Then, spontaneously offered accounts are explored. These accounts, and the responses they elicited, make visible additional incompatible community beliefs about how one ought to be intellectual.

In Chapter 4, I explore how questioning and responding have implications for situationally desired and disvalued aspects of being intellectual. The chapter considers how uses of marked and unmarked questions, time references, interest queries, and lexical choices that unmask backgrounded intellectual frames are used to challenge (and support) different aspects of intellectual identity.

Chapter 5 examines how issues of personal character become relevant in discussion. In discussion of topics that are "decision-making implicative," certain underlying questions come into play. In such discussions, it becomes relevant to ask whose material interests are being served, as well as about the morality and practicality of what is being proposed. Morality, practicality, and interests, I argue, are inescapably character challenges, and while a presenter's intellectual distance from a topic can decrease the seriousness of the challenge, it cannot eliminate it. In addition, the ways in which a challenge gets interlocked with a counterchallenge are explored.

In part II, dilemmas and discourse practices of the academic colloquium are examined from the group perspective. Chapter 6 draws on the
interviews at University X to make visible two ways the "equality-expertise"
dilemma identified by Billig and his colleagues (Billig et al., 1988) is
instantiated in the academic colloquium. The interviews evince that academics believe that ideas should be considered on their own merit, and that
they should be examined in line with a speaker's expertise. In addition,
many interviewees believed that everyone should be willing to participate,
but only those who were knowledgeable should talk.

Chapter 7 examines how institutional rank, an indirect indicator of
expertise as well as a marker of inequality, is displayed discursively. I describe
how talk and silence, question types, and admission of not comprehending,
tag a person as either a graduate student or a faculty member. In addition, I
show how State U's "five minute rule," introduced to combat inequality,
nonetheless became part of the group structure that supported it.

Chapter 8 examines group beliefs about the role of emotion in intellectual talk. Academics' routine formulation of the appropriate role—passion about ideas is good; hostility toward people is bad—is shown to rest
on a problematic assumption. Drawing on the interviews at both universities, we see that while academics frequently talk as if ideas and people can
be separated, they know that they cannot. Then, academics' beliefs about
the values of storytelling, personal anecdotes, and joking are examined,
revealing yet other interactional dilemmas.

In chapter 9 the discursive characteristics and situational framing
choices that facilitated a sense of community at State U are described.
Community, I assert in chapter 9, and argue explicitly in chapter 10, is
the central means through which groups seek to minimize the potential
problems of too little passion or too much hostility. Identified are several
conversational practices that contributed to the State U sense of community. In addition, I show how the group's use of humor and its framing of participation as "obligatory voluntarism" aided State U's
achievement of community.

The final section (part III) moves toward a philosophical and pragmatic
reconstruction of practice, and draws out theoretical and methodological
implications. In chapter 10, three proposals are put forward about how
academic colloquia could be improved. The first proposal addresses issues
of group structure and design, and develops the explicit argument for the
link between intellectual community and discussion quality. The second
proposal advances a dilemmatic ideal for how participants should talk.
Academics are shown to have contradictory beliefs about what constitutes
good discussion. These contrary beliefs, "discussion as dialectic" and "discussion as constructive criticism," I suggest, are best understood as horns
of an interactional dilemma that should guide academics' thoughts about

how to act. The third proposal focuses on how academics should talk with each other about colloquia in which they have participated. The chapter concludes by sketching the likely scope of the proposals.

Chapter 11, "Epilogue," eavesdrops on an imagined discussion at the State U colloquium in which the group talks about the book (i.e., the first ten chapters). Questions about potential implications for approaching social inquiry, future communicative theorizing, and academic conduct furnish the discussion frame for the group, and the group's conversation forms the book's conclusion.

I

Participant Dilemmas

2

Dilemmas of Identity

Excerpt 1

Obviously you think it's [the departmental colloquium] a good thing to study because things happen there that are curious and of interest . . . It's a good place where egos are on the line . . . and how people present themselves matters really. And I resent that at some level because I just want it to be a place where people just come in, think it's exciting for people to do research, say what's on their minds. (faculty member comment to interviewer)

Explicit in this faculty member's comment, although bemoaned as a sad state of affairs, is the belief that identity concerns do not get left at the door when people participate in intellectual discussion. Rather, identity concerns influence talk in interesting and significant ways. Consider, then, how State U participants understood their colloquium's purpose, and what their concerns were as presenters and discussants.

THE COLLOQUIUM PURPOSE

State U interviewees were first asked to describe the purpose of their weekly colloquium. Rich, a faculty member, stated the purpose this way:

Excerpt 2

Well, the purpose of colloquium is to provide uh, an institutionalized vehicle for uh, the graduate students and faculty to come together, uh around issues of common concern, trade ideas, whatever, learn things, uh have some common objects of analysis for discussion, uh develop a sense of community, that's basically it.

Present in most participants' initial characterizations were group-level formulations. That is, people articulated as goals the desired outcomes expected to result from people collectively engaging in talk. Two outcomes were repeatedly mentioned: (a) the development of ideas, and (b) the building of intellectual community. Both of these are present in Rich's description. These same two group goals are visible in other faculty responses. Chris saw the colloquium's purpose as "a kind of ideal of academic community" where there is "an ongoing discussion of issues, uhm development of perspectives, uh, cooperation in the search for truth." Faculty member Mary, described the colloquium as a place that provided an opportunity "to see how we collectively think." A graduate student said colloquium "tries not to complete ideas but to further ideas in a more familiar setting."

These characterizations of group goals provide an immediately recognizable picture of State U's colloquium as intellectual discussion. What they do *not* provide is any sense of how individuals are expected to act. By describing the goals of the colloquium in this way—not specifying any difficulties that face participants as they try to achieve them—interviewees implicitly treated individual involvement as unproblematic. Yet, when interviewees formulate their concerns as presenters and discussants, worries about their own identities, and to a lesser extent others', become central.

PRESENTER CONCERNS

The most noticeable concern of presenters was to be seen as intellectually able. In response to a question about likely concern of presenters, Frank, a faculty member said:

Excerpt 3

I think there's a concern about appearing intelligent, appearing like you know you're doing something worthwhile and that you're doing a fairly good job of it.

Graduate students voiced this concern as well. Sally said she would be concerned when presenting as to "whether what I have to say is worth saying, is important, ah what, 'so what' is the big question." And according to Jen, as a presenter you are concerned about "getting your ideas across for one thing and being competent in getting your ideas across."

Not only did State U interviewees want to be judged intellectually competent, but competence was conceived as tied to particular communicative behaviors, many of which were framed as actions to be avoided. Consider three responses to the question about presenters' likely concerns.

Excerpt 4

Concerns, concerns is the key word there ((laugh)) . . . I think there's a concern about perhaps being taken to task. Uhm, I think there can be concerns about, will the, the, will I get defensive? When people do ask questions I think there's a conscious effort that people say, well they're gonna be tough questions but I don't want this to get to me. (faculty member)

Excerpt 5

My primary goal . . . no matter if just our department's there, or there are people from outside the department, that anyone who's come into the presentation will be able to understand and get something from what I'm saying. I don't think it's always a primary concern of presenters but from my standpoint it always has been, uhm my second ((laughs)) is, has to do with face. And that is that I've covered all the bases? And that I've anticipated questions that I might be asked so that if I'm asked question, a question, that I'm not sitting there with egg on my face saying "Ah well that's an interesting position and I'm certainly going to look into it." Because then I've lost face. (graduate student)

Excerpt 6

Same kinds of concerns I have any time I'm presenting, doing any sort of formal presentation. Uhm, start with the basic Dan Quayle sorts of things. I don't want to drool and fall over. Ah I don't want to say that Columbus discovered America in 1942. Uh, and, but also uhm, you know, I want, I'm hop-, I'm hoping to get people to ah, to, I'm trying to persuade people of some of the points I'm trying to make. Uhm I'm trying to get them interested in what I'm doing. (faculty member)

Presenters cared about how others saw them. They wanted to get their facts straight, be clear about ideas, be articulate, have interesting things to say, and answer questions well. Being competent meant more than doing appropriate actions, however; it involved avoiding "drooling and falling over," "getting egg on my face" and letting discussion "get to me."[1] Of note is how these descriptions give failure an emotional vividness absent from the more matter-of-fact descriptions of what participants hoped to accomplish. Yet, although both faculty and graduate students expressed self-presentational qualms, it was not with the same intensity or about the same things.

In response to a question about how graduate student and faculty concerns might differ, two participants said the following:

Excerpt 7

I think faculty have to deal a lot less with whether their ideas are going to even be acceptable or not. Where students are at that beginning level where their ideas are even getting considered, accepted, or whether they're going to be laughed at . . . Faculty presentations are much more advanced . . . it's more whether they're gonna present it well, or whatever. And whether they're advanced enough. (graduate student)

Excerpt 8

I think graduate students would be more concerned about the things I just mentioned [being evaluated] because their careers aren't made. They're coming up with new ideas and most of the faculty have had some strokes for ideas so if they have a couple bad ones, ((laugh)) it doesn't matter. But graduate students have to prove they have good ones. (faculty member)

Being a presenter at colloquium was feared by graduate students more intensely than by faculty. Faculty and graduate students, alike, saw graduate students' performance as more consequential for the individual's standing in the community. Graduate students had to prove they were capable of good ideas; faculty members, in contrast, had that presumption in their favor. And although a faculty member's performance over time

---

1. In acknowledging self-presentational concerns, participants expressed discomfort. This is most visible in the graduate student's (Excerpt 5) mention of her "second" concern, introduced with a laugh that is hard to hear as other than embarrassed. It is also visible in the faculty member's joke (Excerpt 4) about the interviewer's question wording, "Concerns, concerns is the key word there laugh." This discomfort arises I would argue because group-level formulations delegitimate people having concerns about themselves, particularly if those concerns involve personal fears.

could problematize this presumption, it was unlikely to be overturned by his or her actions in a single situation.

This difference in identity stakes was played out as different interactional foci.

Excerpt 9

I think that I would imagine for graduate students the concern of not making a fool out of themselves is higher than, ah, their concern about persuading people uh, uhm to go along with their perspective. (faculty member)

Excerpt 10

Let's distinguish between our faculty members and our students. I think for the faculty who have been around here for awhile and for whom it's no longer a maiden voyage to make a presentation, they're typically interested in displaying their area and also in provoking interest. (faculty member)

Trying to avoid looking foolish and seeking to provoke interest are negatively related activities. Each emphasizes a different approach to presentation and discussion. Just as a soccer team that is attending to defending its own goal is going to be doing different things from an offensive one, so too with colloquium presenters. That is, the conversational moves that minimize the likelihood of looking stupid are bad choices if one is also trying to provoke interest. As in soccer, the most skilled players engage in moves that conventional wisdom would describe as unsafe. On the other hand, a sure way to display incompetence is to pursue high-risk moves and repeatedly fail.

Ably presenting intellectual work challenges academics of all ranks, but given graduate students' more limited experiences, this type of academic presentation is a more pressing challenge to them. Not only is coming up with something intellectually newsworthy a challenge—an issue with which faculty members also struggle—but the possibility of appearing ignorant of an important issue, or making a foolish claim, is a danger that demands careful monitoring. In this institutional context, where evaluation and ranking are endemic, students need to avoid verbal actions that lead to being written off. At the same time, the further along students are in their course of study, the more crucial it becomes to show more than minimal competence. If students are to become permanent residents of academe, an end goal many have, they need to move beyond intellectually defensive moves (making small safe claims, avoiding interesting ideas that might reveal confusion) and engage in the riskier moves of self-assertion. They must, in one senior faculty member's words, show that they are "confident enough, or competent enough in their own minds, uh, to risk themselves, and I mean really risk themselves."

DISCUSSANT CONCERNS

Although the concern to appear intellectually competent was more highlighted in interviewees' talk about the presenter role, it was visibly present for the discussant role as well. When asked whether participants did any comment-editing, a graduate student acknowledged that he worked at "making the question seem more intelligent so to say than just a simple little question" and a faculty member stated that he didn't "want to ask a silly question or make a silly statement." One prominent face concern of discussants, then, was to appear intellectually competent.

Another identity concern that coexisted with this one, although not acknowledged in a straightforward way, was a concern to not be seen as *trying* to be seen as smart. Put somewhat differently, while people wanted to be seen as smart, they wanted to avoid appearing as if they were concerned about displaying their intellectual prowess. This second concern was one that participants did not claim for themselves, but was visible in their implied criticisms of others' actions. It was also a concern more prominent for faculty than for students.

Consider the response of a faculty member when asked if the colloquium served any "unofficial purposes."

Excerpt 10

One of the purposes it serves is to give different people, ah I think more faculty than graduate students, a chance to kind of show that *they*'re smart, sometimes by showing that someone else isn't as smart as *they* are.

Another faculty member concluded his comment about unofficial purposes saying "I think that there's a definite ego function involved. . . . I would prefer if it weren't going on." Thus we see a contrast between the way participants describe their own concerns, and how they talk about others ("they"). Participants matter-of-factly acknowledged their concern to be viewed as intellectually competent but described others as behaving in "show-off" and "ego-oriented" ways. These descriptors are not positive. Given their relevance to this talk occasion, it is reasonable to presume that participants were concerned *not* to have these labels attached to self.

Putting the two together suggests that the central face concern of discussants was to be seen as intellectually able without being seen as a show-off.

To describe the communicative behaviors that discussants regarded as effective in realizing this rather complex identity concern, it is necessary to consider specific features of the other being addressed. In the interviews, participants identified two primary types of information about the other that were expected to influence communicative behavior: (a) a person's status and (b) his or her ability to "take it."[2]

The most important factor was status. Both faculty and students at State U expected differences in status to have an effect on individual worries in the colloquium. One faculty member commented:

Excerpt 12

Your status or reputation is on the line in that situation and so you know that's why I say probably the farther down you go in the hierarchy, ya know from full professor to beginning graduate student, uh the more scary the situation is from that point of view.

A junior faculty member talking about his role stated that "there needs to be some recognition of boundaries and differences." Participants felt that the lower the status of the presenter, in comparison to that of the questioner, the less "harsh" or critical a discussant's comments should be. Faculty member Chris says:

Excerpt 13

I exercise tact in uh formulating things, uh I think that in, I have a concern and again this is a concern that is more prominent sort of the lower the status of the person presenting.

When asked if he ever edited his comments, a faculty member said:

[2.] A third factor was mentioned by participants as influencing the way they talked. That factor was whether the presenter was inside or outside the departmental community. However, the meaning of this factor was the least elaborated and in many ways most complex. While outsiders were generally treated more politely, this was not always true. If an "outsider" was a good friend/colleague of a departmental member, he or she might be treated as an honorary family member and subjected to the same kind of criticism as insiders. If an "outsider" was a potential faculty member presenting at colloquium as part of an official job interview, he or she usually received tough questioning.

Excerpt 14

If I think that the question may embarrass the student or may seem too harsh
I will phrase it more, edit it in a way that makes it less [harsh]. I think that I
would be less likely to do that with faculty.

A second factor that influenced participants' beliefs about appropriate
behavior involves the other's ability to "take it." This factor was not as clearly
defined as status, yet judging this accurately seemed to be important in the
colloquium. Ability to take it seemed to be related to status, but was not the
same. It appeared to include assessments of interactive style as well as intellectual ability. James described the colloquium as "a discussion or forum in
which people have different levels of competence," and participants
stressed that this needed to be considered in formulating comments.
    Another faculty member argued that participants

Excerpt 15

have to be willing to put ideas on the line and get feedback and learn how to
take that constructively uhm and a lot of people, for a lot of people that's a
very difficult thing to do.

Not only did people vary in their ability to take it, but the higher status
members (i.e., faculty members), especially, were supposed to take this
level of ability into consideration in formulating their comments. A graduate student commented:

Excerpt 16

I think the faculty has a general idea of who's who and who is doing what,
who can take what so to say, uhm so I have seen them address different people in the colloquium in different ways. I have seen them be much easier on
some people than others. They tend to adapt for the most part I'd have to
say, especially this year, they adapt fairly well this year.

To summarize, participants were expected to take account of another's
institutional rank and ability to "take it" in offering comments. Presenters
who were of low institutional rank and/or limited interactive ability were
to be questioned with greater gentleness and politeness than was expected
for people who were not. But how much gentler and how much more
polite? How did these rules dovetail with individual identity concerns and
group purposes?

Discussants wanted to display intellectual competence while avoiding being seen as egotistical. They pursued this identity concern while attending to the institutional goals of advancing ideas and cultivating community. In doing so, discussants faced a dilemma when they formulated questions to be addressed by the presenter. A fierce pursuit of another's claim could be seen as supporting intellectual standards and the group goal of advancing ideas, or it could be seen as self-aggrandizing intellectual display. Gentle, nonthreatening questioning could display a commitment to community and a concern not to threaten another's face, or it could be taken as letting poor scholarship go by and/or evidencing intellectual limitations of one or another party. Consider the interview evidence.

First, participants used talk as a way to assess a discussant's intellectual ability. A faculty member commented about fellow participants that "the way they react to issues is a pretty good clue to how they think." In particular, participants who asked tough and challenging questions were seen as smart and competent. This was implicitly cued by what participants sought to avoid, namely, the asking of "nice, little supportive questions," as one faculty member labeled them in jest. Consider faculty member Tom's response to a question about the most active participants:

Excerpt 17

Among the graduate students, the people I think about are Jess, Tim, uh let's see, Felicia will ask a question but it'll be a nice little supportive question.

Implicit in Tom's description of Felicia's participation is a contrast between the unspoken and desirable type of participation—big, tough, challenging questions—and the spoken one. Tom's characterization not only portrays supportive questions as not desirable, but goes further to suggest that they count questionably, at best, as participation in intellectual discussion. This negative assessment of supportive or information questions is reflected in graduate students' comments as well.

Felicia, for instance, mocked herself for asking a question which "wasn't intellectual at all."

Excerpt 18

Now I did ask a question this semester to ah Professor Davis ah I asked him when his book was coming out, real threatening!((she laughs)). I mean I went out on a limb on that one didn't I! ((laughs)).

Asking tough questions—giving strong criticism—could support the other's identity as intellectually able. An exchange between a faculty member and graduate student that occurred in a classroom, recorded in fieldnotes, illustrates this view of tough criticism. Frank was explaining to Kim, a graduate student, that it does not help *not* to make tough comments in the colloquium. Kim responded by arguing that students "are asked to move up a level and be a colleague" in the colloquium but they "aren't treated like that." She described the "vicious criticism" she received as evidence of this treatment. To this Frank responded by asking, "You think that being a colleague would be different for you?" He told her that being "treated like a graduate student" involves "being pampered."[3] Frank is suggesting that being criticized means that you are respected and taken seriously; it is a sign that your interlocutor sees you as intellectually able.

This view of criticism contrasts with the everyday notion of criticism as an act that is inherently face threatening as well as the view articulated in politeness theory (Brown & Levinson, 1987). Brown and Levinson argue that when a person gives criticism to someone, s/he is questioning that person's competence and thereby threatening his/her positive face. In this community, the understanding of criticism was not so straightforward. While criticism could mean lack of positive regard, it often did not. Rather it was frequently intended, and taken as, an indication that the other *was* competent and intellectually able. Similarly, a lack of criticism did not necessarily mean that a person's work was seen positively; it could mean that a person was seen as intellectually or emotionally unable to manage the criticism. Thus, in this group, criticism carried several meanings, and while it was not always intended or seen as face supportive, it often was.

Graduate students, in fact, were explicitly instructed, as the above example illustrates, to view criticism as indicative of being taken seriously as a scholar. In this way, the colloquium served a socialization function. In this setting faculty could be seen as teaching students to attach this new meaning to criticism, and there is evidence that students came to understand criticism more like the faculty did. One advanced graduate student said:

Excerpt 19

But I think that there, just part of being in this field is getting used to being critiqued or criticized and having your ideas not accepted, or challenged.

[3.] Thanks to Sheryl Baratz for this example.

Getting used to this new meaning of criticism was commented upon by a graduate student in her first year. She described her colloquium role as "to learn how to be a critical audience."

On the other hand, not all students had come to view criticism in this way. In fact, Kim mentioned, in her discussion with Frank, an "underlying support system among graduate students" where "graduate students go [to colloquium] to support fellow graduate students." Sally, another graduate student, confirmed this as she described her role in the colloquium:

Excerpt 20

I'm there to support them, especially for graduate students and um regardless of what the presentation's like, I find myself giving positive feedback, finding something good to say. I know how traumatic it would be for me to be up there.

While faculty seemed to challenge each other relatively freely, students did not. Still, although graduate students felt a need to be careful in asking tough questions of faculty, they saw it as desirable to do so. It was in addressing a faculty member that Wayne reported being concerned with making a question seem more intelligent. Thus, faculty who are described as "sitting in judgment" influenced the communicative behavior of students in complex ways.

Discussants, therefore, faced a dilemma. Asking tough questions could implicate self and other as intellectually able but it could boomerang. If a discussant's questioning revealed that the recipient could not take it, further challenging could being seen as self-serving. Faculty member Frank stated, "If there's too much disagreement then I have some-, occasionally I will not say anything ((Interviewer: why?)) Well because I, I, I am afraid it'll be perceived as too attacking." Frank's formulation points to a negative attribution he seeks to avoid—being too attacking. To say that someone is "too attacking" is to imply that there is a right amount; it suggests the interactional danger lies in going overboard.

The dangers are not just from one direction, however. There is another horn to the dilemma. Participants also need to guard against being "too nice." Not only can niceness suggest that the recipient has limited ability, it may also reflect that a person is letting poor scholarship slip by unchecked. Arthur, a faculty member, explained that "I don't think we should avoid important conflict, particularly intellectual kinds of conflict." In commenting on his own behavior, he goes on to say, "So ya know when he [another faculty member] says things that I disagree with or that I think

are too loose um I, I don't wanta leave him unchallenged." He then artic-
ulates a conflict he experiences:

Excerpt 21

on the one hand I think that it's important to give graduate students an
opportunity with some comfort to talk about ideas and argue about ideas,
um but that's gotta be balanced I think with some sense of ah, of intellectual
integrity that if somebody presents an idea that's really weak or really not
thought through or that someone's got real objections to, they need to be
able to express that.

That being pleasant and uncritical can be problematic is further
attested to by a faculty member. Graduate students, he notes, are not

Excerpt 22

used to being around people who can come down hard on somebody's ideas
but still respect them. And that they don't necessarily understand that push-
ing hard on ideas even though it sounds rough and tumble, it's often the best
way to impr-, better ideas.

I would suggest that a good intellectual community for State U respon-
dents was one in which people felt comfortable to speak, a group climate
that was facilitated when people felt they would not be humiliated. At the
same time, the group goal of advancing ideas required people to give serious scrutiny and strong criticism to each other's claims, an activity that
could cause humiliation.

The communicative challenge for participants in this setting was to
design comments for specific others that were seen as appropriate. This
was no easy task, for the group belief about what counted as appropriate
contained injunctions about communicative action that, while not necessarily contradictory, were in tension.

ATTRIBUTION-MAKING
IN INTELLECTUAL DISCUSSION

The interviews provide a picture of the concerns of graduate students and
faculty at State U. In this section, I propose a more general model of how
identity judgments will be made in academic discussions where one person

has presented his or her ideas to a group, and then the group discusses those ideas.[4] A first part of making attributions about discussants and presenters, I would suggest, is to make judgments about the discussant's question and its response. While discussants do not always use the interrogative form, comments typically have the demand characteristic of a question. That is, given the presentation-discussion format, at the end of a discussant's comment is an unstated question to the presenter asking "What do you think of what I just said?" Thus, discussion following an academic presentation is conceived as consisting of questions and responses.

Three judgments are expected to be made about questions and responses. A first judgment is about the difficulty of the question asked; that is, how easy or tough is it? What does it require of the presenter in terms of an answer? As the interviews suggested, questions that ask for clarification or elaboration are generally regarded as easy. Questions or comments that require more from the recipient are tougher.[5] Question difficulty will be a judgment influenced by an observer's knowledge and understanding of the topic under discussion. The more expert an observer is in a subject, the more his or her judgment is expected to be consistent with that of other experts; the more novice an observer, the less predictable would be his or her judgment of question difficulty. Thus, while all observers are expected to assess question difficulty, the assessments they reach will not necessarily be the same.

In addition to question difficulty, a second judgment is made: Is the question fair? While the assessment of difficulty is tied primarily to topical knowledge and the intellectual complexity of the question, the judgment of fairness is made by considering whether there is a reasonable match between the socially understood identity of the presenter and the assessed toughness of the question. Factors likely to influence an observer's situated judgment of fairness include: (a) individual observer assessments of what questions might reasonably be asked of participants at certain status levels and abilities, and (b) general community expectations about the importance of avoiding the embarrassment of participants, versus a commitment to lively, pointed, and critical discussion.

[4.] Not all intellectual discussions involve presentations. Some involve discussion of a book or article to which no group member has special ties. Others emerge spontaneously among several individuals in informal nonpublic settings. Whether a discussion is public or private, or about intellectual issues connected primarily to one party, are important differences that could be expected to affect how people draw inferences about each other. This proposed model is outside of what would typically be considered attribution research (see Ross & Fletcher, 1985; Seibold & Spitzberg, 1982), but is consistent with recent work in social psychology that seeks to develop a discourse analytic approach to attribution (Antaki, 1994; Edwards & Potter, 1992)

[5.] The issue of what counts as "more demanding" is explored in Chapters 4 and 5.

A final judgment observers will make concerns the adequacy of the response to the question. A judgment that a recipient has responded adequately is an assessment that he or she has handled the question suitably. For instance, adequacy may involve a straightforward answer but it could also involve refusing to answer a question, challenging what is presupposed, querying an implied definition of terms, and so on. Whether a response is judged adequate will depend on the assessed appropriateness of the response to the question. Such a judgment is one about which observers will not necessarily agree. Like that about question difficulty, the judgment of response adequacy will be influenced by expertise level, but it is also likely to be influenced by beliefs an observer holds about a recipient's responsibility to address the question posed, versus a recipient's right to reframe a question.

Judgments about these three issues become the basis upon which attributions are made. If a question is asked that is perceived to be tough and fair, and the response is adequate, then both the discussant and the recipient are seen to be intellectually able. This state is in fact the ideal of intellectual discussion—ideas are being advanced, tested, and criticized; intellectual community is being maintained—and at the same time each party is implicitly supporting self's and other's face concerns to be intellectually able. In this situation, the definition of intellectual conversation offered by Dabbs (1985) is most applicable: "Ideas are more central than personal relationships" (p. 183). Even here identity concerns are operative, although achieved in a way that does not call into question commitment to the group goals. Hence, when the group goals are accomplished, individual identity concerns are unmarked and less visible (see Table 1).

Discussion does not always proceed smoothly, however. Questions are not always tough and fair; responses are not always adequate. When they are not, a negative attribution will be made about one or both parties. If a question is perceived as unfair, the asker will be judged as self-serving. If a response is inadequate, there will be concerns about the presenter's intellectual competence: milder concerns if the question is perceived tough or unfair, more serious ones if the question is judged easy and fair. If the question is perceived to be easy, the attributional picture will be the most ambiguous for presenter and discussant. This is so because there are multiple reasons why easy questions are posed.

Identity attributions are not made and fixed within a single exchange; rather, they occur across exchanges. In general, the more history people have with each other, the less important any single exchange is for attributions. This is one reason that colloquium presentations are more consequential for graduate students than for faculty members. Furthermore, judgments about a person are not made in a strict sequential order, where assessments of questions are made prior to, and independent of, actual

Table 1. The Attribution Process in Intellectual Discussion

	Question-Response Assessments			Attribution Outcomes	
	Question difficulty	Question fairness	Response	Discussant	Presenter
1.	Tough	Fair	Adequate	Int. able	Int. able
2.	Tough	Unfair	Adequate	Able but self-serving	Int. able
3.	Tough	Fair	Inadequate	Int. able	Int. limited
4.	Tough	Unfair	Inadequate	Int. able self-serving	Indet.
5.	Easy	Fair	Adequate	Indet. /int. limited	Indet.
6.	Easy	Fair	Inadequate	Indet. /int. limited	Int. limited
7.	Easy	Unfair	Inadequate	Indet. /self-serving	Int. limited

Note. Because the judgments of question difficulty, fairness and response adequacy are made concurrently, it is not possible to judge a question, easy, unfair, and adequate. Perceivers will either judge the Q-R sequence to be (6) or (7). An "easy unfair" question would be one that asks for information participants of a presenter's rank would be expected to possess where it is known that the specific presenter does not possess the information that the question requests. Indet. = indeterminate; int.limited = intellectually limited; int. able = intellectually able.

responses. Instead, actual responses are filtered through existing perceptions. Assessments of questions and responses influence attributions made about participants, but judgments about the question-response sequence are influenced, in turn, by prior information about participants' identities. In sum, this is a cycle that includes questions, responses, and participants; each has implications for the other components.

One feature of this model worth noting is its ability to account for what is a common phenomenon in academic discussions—that various participants can walk away from a discussion holding quite different assessments of each other's intellectual ability and "egotism." This is possible because the grounds on which assessments of intellectual ability and egotism are made rest on judgments that are socially constituted ("toughness," "fairness," "adequacy") and linked only loosely to objective criteria.

In colloquium, State U participants faced dilemmas. As presenters they could pursue a high-risk but relatively desirable identity of being intellectually provocative, or they could strive for a more achievable but less valued identity: avoiding serious intellectual errors. As discussants, participants were expected to support by challenging, but challenge without threatening. Consider now how these dilemmas get played out in colloquium talk.

3

Positioning And Accounting

Tim mounts the stairs to the seminar room deliberating about what he should say in opening. "This paper extends the work of my dissertation that recently appeared in the journal of—No, sounds like I have everything sorted out. This paper is my first attempt to—No, too wimpy."

POSITIONING SELF

The presentation of one's own thinking is an inherently risky activity. As one faculty member put it, "That's what you're doing, is presenting part of yourself." While everybody may be presenting part of self, not everyone is presenting the same amount of self. How closely presenters align with their ideas differs considerably. This choice is consequential because it is a major way presenters instruct others how they see self, and how they expect others to treat them.

At one end of a continuum, presenters align themselves closely with a set of ideas or issues. Tying ideas closely to self is visible when a speaker references a large amount of time and energy that she has invested in the ideas; it is also marked by reference to the socially valued tangible by-products of involvement with ideas. Consider, for instance, what Trent, a faculty speaker from outside the department, says, following an introduction that included the fact that he had several grants and had recently published a book.

Excerpt 23

Thank you Jim, Trent's the name, religion's my game, *those of you who are graduate students,* uh sometimes if you want a little reflection on what happens when events drive your interests, you know, and sorta you get a hold of a topic that won't seem to go away, that's been my experience with uh, with religion. The book, uh, was uh based on research I was involved in while still a graduate student and then a postdoctoral at {Y University} uh where we had a major grant to do a study of electronic church broadcasting, Pat Robertson, the 700 club, the Jimmy Swaggart style of broadcasting. And as part of that I uh conducted my own research that culminated in my dissertation and then worked much of that data into the book, and that was the book. What I want to talk about today is something completely different. It's looking also at issues of mass media and religion but from another perspective, from the other side as it were. Uh I have a grant from the Brandon endowment a large uh foundation in the East, in Baltimore, to do a study of how uh secular press, and particularly they're interested in daily newspapers . . .

In the opening of his talk, Trent establishes himself as a highly experienced academic. He does this in a humorous and solidarity-building way, by referring to events that mark novice status—being a graduate student—as being sometime in the past. Trent also does this by referring to products (a book, grants) that are generally seen as evidence of intellectual skill, something that can be produced only by sustained involvement. In his opening comments, then, Trent claims a high level of intellectual ability. In doing so, we see him implicitly licensing the most difficult of questions. Any question should be fair game for someone who has thought long and hard about a set of ideas. Thus, an initial claim to high ability level allows no attribution out for a presenter during the discussion period. If the presenter answers inadequately, he or she will be judged to have intellectual limitations.

Not all speakers are prepared to align self as closely with the ideas they are presenting. Consider Beth, a faculty member of roughly similar rank, who introduces a talk about "face and facework" in this way:

Excerpt 24

What you're going to hear about today is a paper in process—now one can ask what are the face implications of saying "in process"? ((group laughter)) No but I'm hoping that I can get a lot of good feedback, criticism here because I'll be reworking it the next uh, month or so and it'll be a chapter coming out in . . .[1]

[1.] This quotation was taken from a presentation I gave. While I have generally avoided selecting my own talk, I do include several instances to mark my membership in the group whose practices I am seeking to understand.

Unlike Trent, Beth is a department member of the colloquium group being studied. This inside status is visible in the brevity of her opening contextualizing remarks; a brevity warranted if people already know her well. In her opening remarks, Beth creates more distance between herself and the ideas she is presenting than Trent did. While she implicitly claims high ability—she is writing a chapter for a highly visible book—she highlights that she is not completely behind the ideas she is presenting; the ideas are "in process." Through use of this phrase, she licenses herself to change her mind and not to defend everything she says. This phrase also functions to instruct others not to be overly tough in their questioning. That this in fact is what it means to mark something in process is humorously alluded to in her answer to the rhetorical question she poses about the face implications of using that phrase. Her answer, "No, but I'm hoping I can get a lot of good feedback, criticism," partially overturns that implication but at the same time makes it apparent that she sees certain potential questions at a difficulty level that it would be unfair to expect her to have worked through. Thus we see Beth doing more work to insure that inadequate answers will not reflect negatively on her intellectual ability.

Presenters use, in fact, a whole set of stock phrases that draw upon temporal and spatial metaphors to convey that they have been involved with the ideas being presented for only a short time ("a pilot study," "in the beginning stages," "in progress") or that the ideas are tangential to self's concerns ("a spin-off of" "a tangent of the main project"). In the interviews conducted at University X, a faculty member spontaneously commented on these phrases:

Excerpt 25

People use a lot of qualification. I mean there's the classic one being, I think, "this is an exploratory study." That's implicitly saying to others: Don't be too critical of this because I haven't worked it out that carefully and I don't wanta take a lot of shit . . . and I guess on the other end, things that don't qualify but enhance, uh, when you start out you could say, you know, I spent a lot of years on this or something like that . . . but it also entails risk because if somebody really doesn't like it then I think the threat itself is greater.

While the positioning of self to ideas often draws upon relatively standard phrases and lines of argument, it can also be done in novel ways. Consider Frank's opening comment after he had been introduced as someone who had been on sabbatical the previous semester. In introducing him, James had read from a flyer that described who was speaking on what topic. Frank says:

Excerpt 26

Uh, in fact I want, I want this for a prop, ((holding the flyer)) I was gonna say, uh I think these uh flyers they're sending around, that they're sending around this semester are really nice but uh I must say it kinda ups the ante a little bit on these colloquia, you know it's like in the old days they would say Frank is going to talk about history and you would just come in and talk about history but now ((pause, then in a reading voice)) Professor Frank G. Ellison is going to present a lecture on ((pause)) reconstructing, like WOW, I better have something together for this. ((group laughter))

Besides highlighting the way self is on the line for ideas, Frank's comments can be seen as reframing the activity that he wants to be seen as doing. By explicitly problematizing the activity he is engaged in—"lecturing" versus "talking"—Frank implicitly increases the legitimacy of the more informal mode, a mode of talk that permits lower levels of clarity from a competent presenter.

Thus far I have focused on the talk of faculty but similar conversational moves are seen in the talk of graduate students. In presenting a required Ph.D. colloquium paper, Brenda introduced it by noting, "This paper I'm going to talk about today grew out of a seminar on theory and practice that I took summer before last with Ken Freesen" and went on to add in introducing the particular author upon which the paper focused, "Now like many of you I first came upon this work in a class I took with Tim Falcon." Like Trent, Brenda refers to certain parts of graduate school being in the past and identifies the ideas as having some longevity (the paper grew out of a seminar). Brenda's comments thus establish her identity claim on the novice-expert continuum. Through the references to classwork she establishes herself as a student (on the novice end) but at the same time makes clear that she is not a beginner.

While graduate students did do conversational work to show their involvement with ideas, they frequently went to considerable lengths to create distance between self and the ideas they were presenting. Consider Ruth's opening comments in the presentation of the paper she used to satisfy the departmental requirement for Ph.D. students:

Excerpt 27

Thank you, Rich, uh first of all, I'd like to begin by thanking the faculty for reviewing my manuscript and giving me so many nice criticisms and suggestions. ((group laughter)) Uh, I know it's your job ((group laughter)) but I also know that my paper came at the time . . . I hope that I've addressed your criticisms and suggestions as best as I can.

Notable in Ruth's opening is a sense that she sees what she is doing as completing a task given to her by external agents whose specifications she is trying to meet. This is especially highlighted by her referencing of the obligations in the faculty-student role—faculty are required to give feedback; students are expected to use it to improve. This task framing, while certainly a reasonable one in the situation, de-emphasizes Ruth's own investment with the ideas. Ruth continues to mark a distance between self and ideas in responses to questions about her work. For instance, in response to a question from a faculty member, Ruth says, "Well that was one of the problems with the paper" and "I guess you'd say my argument was confounded with. . . ." Ruth's description of her argument using the past tense makes sense only if she is talking about an argument *in the paper* rather than the argument she is making right then in the discussion situation. This, along with her explicit reference to her own ideas as "the paper," frame her as the paper's spokesperson rather than highlighting her authorship of the ideas.[2] There are several plausible motives for Ruth's behavior. One possibility is that Ruth is trying to appease her faculty mentors and show them that she recognizes her dependency and their more knowledgeable status. Another possibility, not necessarily incompatible with the first, is that Ruth is creating a distance between self and ideas to minimize the impact of criticism and ward off negative identity attributions. Whatever the particular motivation, the moves mark her as a novice, someone who is not identifying with ideas in the ways expected of a full-fledged academic.

To summarize, presenters in intellectual discussion make clear how invested they are in their ideas. In framing their investment, they face a dilemma. Higher degrees of investment carry a potential for higher reward but at the same time are highly risky. This trade-off is articulated in a graduate student's response to an interview question about participants' likely concerns during colloquia:

Excerpt 28

If their [students'] work is really fully developed they've invested a lot into it and this is probably their work, their dissertation, you know this is what their

---

[2.] Goffman (1981) introduced the idea of "footing" to distinguish among ambiguities within the speaker role. Speakers in conversation are usually *animators* (the person actually speaking), *authors* (composers of the words), and *principals* (person who is committed to what the words say). While the three often go together, it is possible to separate these three facets of the speaker role. Hill and Irvine (1993) consider an interesting array of cross-cultural situations where this happens. In this instance Ruth could be described as presenting herself as an animator rather than the principal.

whole degree is resting on. So I think probably the further developed along it is, the more concerns they would have that it would be accepted, you know, that if it was to them just a work in progress, it wouldn't be as traumatic to have it challenged quite a bit as if, you know, they had been spending a great deal of time developing it and thought they were near the end and then just, you know, torn apart.

Through their opening remarks, presenters position themselves in relation to their ideas. Through the host of conversational devices identified above, as well as others, presenters inform audiences about how much they see self as being responsible for the ideas about which they talk. A low level of responsibility licenses less able discussion performance but simultaneously implies that the presenter has less knowledge, experience, and, perhaps, ability. A high level of responsibility suggests a high level of intellectual competence. It also sets up an expectation that the presenter can handle difficult questions and comments. Should a presenter not do so, he or she is especially high risk for being seen as pretentious and/or intellectually incompetent.

In making position claims, presenters face a difficult balancing act. Presenters want to establish themselves as intellectually competent. Such an identity seems accomplished best by a high initial claim to intellectual ability. Yet there are serious costs if a presenter claims a high level and fails to perform at that level. Not only does the person discredit his or her situated claim to high ability; he or she also calls into question basic judgment skills. That is, I would suggest that participants in intellectual discussion are expected not to overestimate their knowledgeability and/or argumentative competence, but a minimal claim to intellectual competence, while much less difficult to support, is self-limiting. Furthermore, the higher the institutional status of the person, the more a limited intellectual competence claim may call into question the presenter's suitability to be in the institutional position that he or she occupies.

PARTICIPANT ACCOUNTS

Examination of another category of talk—accounts and disclaimers (e.g., Cody & McLaughlin, 1990; Hewitt & Stokes, 1975; Scott & Lyman, 1968; Semin & Manstead, 1983)—provides another lens on a community's beliefs about what it means to be intellectually competent. Accounts (and disclaimers) inform us in a particularly vivid fashion what a person believes the community holds to be appropriate or desirable behavior. An apology, an excuse, or a justification implies that the person sees as problematic the question of whether he or she has lived up to a community standard. Thus, when we see people offering accounts, we have an especially good window into their minds; we have strong evidence of what identity concerns a person must have. Without a belief that they may have done something seen as wrong in others' eyes, the conversational work done to ward off others from thinking that they routinely act that way would make no sense.

From a certain perspective, accounting is what intellectual discussion is all about; questioners ask presenters to justify and supply reasons for what they claim. The next chapter considers this broad kind of accounting work, pervasive in questioning and responding. Here, I focus on spontaneous acts of accounting that surfaced in presenters' and discussants' talk as they pursued particular topical foci. Spontaneous accounts surfaced in two primary areas: (a) researcher choices in topic and method, and (b) a person's situated communicative style. Examination of these accounts points to three additional sets of tensions participants face.

Researcher Choices

In disciplines within the human sciences, most topical areas of research can be characterized in terms of both what they succeed in doing and what they fail to do. Within the field of communication, good research is theoretically interesting and practically useful. However, as is often the case, criteria pull in antagonistic directions. Research that succeeds in addressing the everyday world and its problems is more likely to fail to speak to the developing intellectual puzzles within the disciplinary community. On the other hand, research that succeeds in addressing theoretical interests of the academic discipline, risks being seen as irrelevant to practical concerns (Craig, 1995).

Words and phrases exist within academic communities that convey how an individual scholar's work is being judged. Words like *pedestrian, atheoretical,* or even *applied* mark the research (and the researcher) as giving insufficient attention to theoretical concerns; terms like *esoteric, ivory towerish,* or *abstract theorizing* convey that work has been insufficiently attentive to people's communicative practices. That this tension exists, and that participants are concerned to place themselves and their work in a place that avoids one or other of these attributions, are made visible in people's spontaneous disclaimers.

For instance, consider Art's embedded disclaimer in Excerpt 29, which is the end of a long answer to a previously posed question.

Excerpt 29

and so on a very, on the very pragmatic or practical level and I know, you know, it's problematic in a university setting to talk very much about research having practical outcomes and practical applications and uh *I'm not all that interested in doing practical research usually myself* but I think that will be a sort of a practical, pragmatic outcome. Uhm on a more theoretical level . . .

In an earlier part of his answer, not fully displayed in Excerpt 29, Art has highlighted the practical usefulness of his work. In concluding his answer, however, he interrupts himself with an aside about the perceived disvaluing of practical work in the university setting, and his "typical" relationship to practical research. How do we make sense of his disclaimer that he is not usually practical in the middle of an explicit argument that his work is practically useful? Such a conversational move, I would suggest, only makes sense if a speaker is attempting to navigate between conflicting identity concerns. Yes, Art is "practical"—his research speaks to important everyday problems; no Art is not "practical"—his intellectual interests are not pedestrian or atheoretical.

Besides topical disclaimers, graduate students and faculty gave accounts and made disclaimers for data and methodology choices. Excerpt 30 was produced by a graduate student in the middle of his presentation about a television preacher; Excerpt 31 is part of a faculty visitor's answer to a question/suggestion about likely directions in studying conflicts people have.

Excerpt 30

The methodology I've used in this study is I looked at six videotapes. One of them is from the fifties, four of them are from the sixties and one of them is from the seventies. *The videotapes weren't chosen for any special reason other than they were available. One of the problems in doing research on {religious preacher's name} is that there is a real poor dating system.* The archives in {city, state} are very disorganized. But I've been able to piece together uh, uh approximate dates and what I'd like to do . . .

Excerpt 31

Oh I think it's a great idea but I haven't figured out how to do it or whether I can do it at this point in time because frankly I don't think that there is a real nice and clean way of describing family environments. You know, what, what would I use to make that judgment? And to what extent could I gather data to make that judgment? And at the same time I'm not sure it would be possible for me to institute that kind of control into the study. Um you know if I get the data collection access I want, what's probably gonna happen is I'm gonna make the best out of what I get and okay, and that's, that' ( ), *and I know that sounds terribly unprofessional but that's the way it is* . . .

In both of these excerpts, the speakers excuse/justify how they are proceeding. Of interest is that the accounts show that each speaker presumes that the audience believes systematic and controlled procedures in research (in sample selection and comparison groups) are important. In verbally marking their actions as potentially problematic, done explicitly in Excerpt 31 ("I know that sounds terribly unprofessional") and more subtly in Excerpt 30 (pointing to the problems in the archives), both speakers display self as methodologically knowledgeable.

While the account (Excerpt 30) and disclaimer (Excerpt 31) point to the speaker's sensitivities that others may see something wrong to have been done, the verbal justification is brief (Excerpt 30) or entirely absent (Excerpt 31). This gives the impression that the speakers do not expect the audience to see the problems as serious ones, that is, these problems require acknowledgment, but do not deserve serious justificatory energy. In a research community, however, how can unsystematic procedures ever be a minor problem?

The answer, I would suggest, lies in the nature of the data with which each presenter is dealing. Each is dealing with naturally occurring communicative interaction. In offering no more than a pro forma justification, the presenters presume that the audience will judge it reasonable for a researcher to sacrifice some degree of methodological systematicity in the service of rich data. That rich data were more important than systematicity in the State U department is further evidenced by (a) the lack of challenge made of these accounts, and (b) the challenge made to speakers who justified the lack of richness in their data in order to be more systematic (see analysis of Excerpt 48).

Communicative Style

Another aspect of intellectual competence involves displaying, or at least showing understanding of, the conversational style that is valued in a community's conduct of intellectual discussion. Consider what the following comments imply about what is valued at State U.

Excerpt 32

It's at least possible to imagine situations in which people judge you as not being particularly competent and yet . . . *Ah, I'm saying that abstractly, because I can't at the moment just think of a great example*

Excerpt 32 tells us that the participant sees it as routinely desirable to give a concrete example of an abstract claim. By highlighting that it is only at the moment that he cannot do so, the speaker excuses his situated failure while simultaneously revealing what he views as the socially understood persona of a good thinker/talker, an identity he claims typically to be.

Excerpt 33

I'm gonna push on what Jim was starting on and I'm not gonna be very linear either.

Excerpt 34

It seems to me, uh, this is kind of, I guess, a series of somewhat connected observations.

Excerpts 33 and 34 illustrate that the speakers see it as necessary to account for their talk as deviating from an understood ideal. Their remarks reveal that they take the ideal intellectual talker to be one who is "linear" and makes observations that are easily and clearly connected. Only if this ideal guides their behavior does it make sense explicitly to label their talk this way. This explicit negative labeling of their own talk displays their intellectual competence; the conversational move both offers evidence that the speakers understand what good intellectual talk should look like, and licenses their rule violation on this occasion.

While most accounts about conversational style were brief prefaces to a substantive remark and elicited no comment from others, this was not always the case. Consider graduate student Rita's initial comment upon concluding her presentation:

Excerpt 35

Rita: Thank you for letting me read this paper. I promise you I'm never gonna do it again ((laugh)) Never, ever ever. I'll never do this again. It's against everything that I teach in a classroom and by God it's terrible to do and I won't do it.

Bill: Why, why did you do it this time?

Rita: Because of all the criticisms. I felt that I should treat this more like a president giving a speech where he was careful with every word he said ((group laugh))

Len: Which president's done that? ((loud group laughter))

In apologizing so extensively, Rita conveys that she sees herself as having violated a community expectation about presentation style: She read a paper and she should have presented extemporaneously. As in Excerpts 33 and 34, her comment both affirms a group expectation and excuses her situated performance (it was atypical and will not happen again). However, in contrast to other spontaneously offered accounts, it is not allowed to pass without comment. When Bill asks her to give a reason for the action for which she had just apologized, he conveys that her action was neither self-evidently understandable nor a minor problem, and while Len's joke about her answer (Which president's done that?) lightens the situation, one is left with a sense of the stylistic trade-offs that State U chose. That is, although State U regarded it as desirable to be articulate, argumentatively organized and have good examples, a speaker who "read" in order to accomplish these conversational features was seen as presenting in an inappropriate fashion. Sacrificing interactional naturalness to be fully coherent and linguistically elegant was judged as going "too far" at State U.

State U did make a distinction between desirable styles in presenting and discussing. Unlike discussing, presenting was an activity for which participants were expected to prepare in advance so that they could talk about ideas and arguments in a clear, organized, and lively fashion. In that sense, presenting and discussing roles brought forward different performance criteria. Identical for both, however, was the expectation that a good style was an argumentatively coherent and linguistically elegant one that did not sacrifice interactional naturalness.

Thus, accounts and their responses reveal how being suitably intellectual is constituted by managing tensions—between being committed to practice and being interested in theory, between being methodologically systematic and pursuing rich data, between linguistic articulateness and interactional naturalness. Moreover, it is at the discourse points at which interactants mark their contributions as faulty that we get an especially clear view of both what is valued and how a community prioritizes among competing values.

4

Questioning and Responding

Excerpt 36

And so uh, the strategy then would be a sort of piling on, an accumulation, bit by bit until finally you were satisfied twenty years later that you were able to say what was going on in this study.

This excerpt comes from a lengthy question addressed to a graduate student presenter in the State U colloquium. This question formulation, as is true of question formulations generally, does a number of different kinds of identity work, including implying how the speaker sees the recipient's scholarly work (and hence the recipient). Within much psychological (e.g., Graesser, 1990; Lehnert, 1978) and educational (e.g., Hunkins, 1989) theorizing, questions have been treated as transparent devices to get information. That questions simultaneously propose and reflect identities of speakers and recipients has largely been ignored. In chapter 7, the link between discussants' questions and their institutional identities is explored;[1] in this chapter the focus is on how academics create intellectual

---

[1.] That status (institutional rank) is cued by discourse choices is perhaps the best established "fact" of the relationship between questioning practices and identity. Exactly how questioning practices will be affected by status relationships is a complex issue and depends on the nature of the situation. Interviews with a president of the United States (Orr, 1980) or high-ranking government officials (Walton, 1989) will yield variation in questioning practices quite different from job interviews (Jablin & Miller, 1990), courtroom exchanges (Penman, 1990) and classroom teaching (Dillon, 1988).

identities through questioning and responding. Analysis of colloquium discourse, in light of the interview findings, suggested that concerns about intellectual identity could be divided into three concerns—being adequately knowledgeable, being an original thinker, and being intellectually sophisticated. For each identity concern, I give evidence of its situational salience and explicate how features of questioning implicated it.

KNOWLEDGEABILITY AND
USE OF MARKED/UNMARKED FORMS

In domains of life in which people are emotionally and/or economically invested, they typically seek to be, and to be seen, as competent. In academia, to be competent is most fundamentally to be knowledgeable. In university settings where discussion is about ideas, to be knowledgeable is far from an easy task. Always, there are more authors to be read, technical information to be mastered, ideas that require understanding and integration into larger frames. In this academic setting, knowledgeability can never be other than bounded and a matter of degree. No person can know everything. Hence, while being a highly knowledgeable person is a desired identity, there is simultaneously a recognition that not knowing, at least under certain circumstances, should be regarded as reasonable.

The judgment of whether it is reasonable (or unreasonable) for a question recipient to know particular information is built into question formulations. As Pomerantz (1988, p. 366) notes, "a speaker unavoidably builds into an information-seeking question an expectation that the recipient should know, may know, probably does not know, etc. the sought-after information." In other words, in the question formulation we see the speaker's assessment of the recipient's knowledgeability level. That this identity-relevant information is routinely present is especially visible when an initial formulation is repaired. Consider the significance in Excerpt 37 of a faculty member's (Roy) reformulation of a question to a graduate student presenter (Sue).

Excerpt 37

Roy: Uhm this is a kinda follow up, I guess on the perceptions thing. *Did you, are you aware, I would assume that,* that studies looking at self attributions and other attributions of competence generally show a pretty high correlation?

Sue: hmm mm

Roy: That, that is generally true? That that person's own self rating of competence correlates pretty highly with ratings of those surrounding?

Roy's question is attempting to get information about the relationship between self-attribution and other-attribution for judgments of interactive competence. Of note is the fact that he begins his question three times using different phrasings each time. From these repairs we can infer that he was dissatisfied in some way with his first two formulations, but what exactly is being repaired?

I suggest that he is dissatisfied with what his initial formulations imply Sue should know. Each formulation implies a different knowledge expectation of Sue. By far the strongest expectation is displayed in the first formulation ("Did you"). Typically, when a speaker begins an utterance, its ending can be projected. If Roy had continued with his initial formulation, it is likely he would have said something like "Did you look at the relationship? . . ." To ask someone if they did something, suggests it is an activity that a reasonable other might expect to be done. This is likely unless a speaker mitigates ("Did you by any chance") or reverses the presumption ("You didn't look at . . ., did you?"). Roy's immediate repair suggests that he does not want to imply that Sue should know what he is asking. His second formulation softens this expectation ("Are you aware"), making it more reasonable if Sue is not able to address the issue. This formulation still conveys, nonetheless, that what is being asked is a kind of information that well-informed others should know. Roy's last formulation ("I assume that studies looking at") conveys the weakest implication that Sue should know the information being asked. It turns the utterance into a statement focused on the question-asker's knowledge rather than into a query directed toward the other. While it does ask her to confirm whether something is true, it sidesteps whether or not she is responsible for having this requested information. Roy's reformulation work, then, gives evidence that at least at some tacit level, speakers recognize the potential identity threat to a person's knowledgeability implied by a question's form.

Question formulations imply whether an asker has a strong or weak expectation that the recipient will be knowledgeable, but not all expectations need to be marked. The unmarked form in such discussions is one in which question formulations rather straightforwardly presume recipient knowledgeability about whatever is being asked about. This presumption is conveyed by the *absence* of mitigators and qualifiers oriented to the issue of knowing.

Excerpt 38

So did, did, in what you said then, does the Inquirer think of themselves as, as in an adversarial relationship with organized religion?

Excerpt 39

So what exactly is a computerized conference in your view?

Excerpt 40

What was it that he was using that, to establish his authority, to keep the authority relationship between him and his audience?

While Excerpts 38 ("in what you said then") and 39 ("in your view") do include conversational markers that make the question less demanding by treating it as a question of opinion rather than fact, neither these two, nor the others, problematize whether the question-recipient will know what is being asked. This, then, is the invisible side of identity work. When presenters supply information to questions whose formulations presume they can do so, question-recipients enact their role as the expert and knowledgeable person in the domain of talk. Should a recipient not know the answer to a question where knowledgeability is presumed, however, he or she will need to do conversational work to overturn a negative identity implication. If successful interactive work is not done, then an implication is left standing that the question recipient has limited knowledge in an area in which another expected fuller knowledge.

That such conversational work gets done is displayed in an exchange between a faculty presenter (Ed) and a faculty discussant (David). Ed has presented a study about religious news coverage in the media. In the discussion period, embedded in a rather lengthy comment, David ask Ed's opinion about a particular body of scholarly literature. Given the absence of mitigators directed to the likelihood of knowing, David's question seems to imply that Ed should be knowledgeable and familiar with authors who write about this literature. As Ed's answer unfolds, it becomes clear that this presumption is not accurate:

Excerpt 41

D: I just am wondering uh how does this relate to {name of literature}, for example, are those in your views, those are reflections of newspaper interests? . . .[2]

[2.] This comment has two kinds of mitigators. The first ("in your views") frames the issue as a matter of opinion rather than fact. This framing gives the answerer more maneuvering room than if it were framed as right/wrong answer. The second mitigator can be seen in the

E: Uh, huh well I, you know it's not something that I've given a great deal of thought to because I, I myself have never been very taken with uh the, what you call {name of specific literature} . . . I haven't thought about this before now but now, being intrigued by the idea, perhaps making, say And, and I'd also have to say that that's a literature I tend not to read a great deal because I haven't found it ( ) I think I got involved in this study originally . . . I'm obviously not a journalist scholar. . . Okay, I'm sorry I mean I just ( ). That's sort of a, of a, of a, of an admission about it. It's not a literature that I have been taken with in the past and it just did not seem to be very fruitful, you know.

Ed is doing considerable work in his answer to justify and make reasonable his lack of familiarity with a literature that David had presumed was related to what he was talking about. In his response, besides accepting responsibility for not knowing ("Okay, I'm sorry"), Ed also suggests that his lack of familiarity exists because of the quality of the literature ("never been very taken," "not seem to be very fruitful"). In characterizing the literature this way, he makes visible an alternative meaning for his not knowing: It's a set of ideas not worth knowing. Whether members of a discussion group treat a presenter's alternative framing as an acceptable reason not to know, or discount it and judge the person to be poorly read and/or deficient in judgment, will depend on individual discussants' personal relationships to, and assessments of, the ideas and authors under discussion.

In the analysis of Excerpt 41, I showed how the presumption of knowledge built into a question's form threatened a recipient. One might conclude from this that if discussants have doubts about whether a recipient knows the answer, their questions will always be less face-threatening if they are formulated to presume the reasonableness of not knowing. This, I contend, is untrue. Just as a question may threaten another's identity by presuming that he or she should know something he or she does not, so too can a question formulation threaten another's identity by assuming that the recipient is unlikely to know something that others regard as part of being competent. Consider the following question posed by a faculty member to a graduate student presenter who has given a talk about the differences between face-to-face interaction and [situation X] type of interaction.

---

opening phrase "I just am wondering." In an unmarked question, there is a presupposition that the question is serious and central to the issue of discussion. Prefacing a question with a "wondering" statement marks it as a spontaneous thought and not necessarily central to the topic at hand. This potentially does two kinds of face work. It marks the question-asker as aware that the question may be tangential, and it recognizes the possibility that the issue may not be a central concern of the speaker. The inability to respond to a question about a marginal topic is less serious than an inability to respond to a central topic.

Excerpt 42

Uh, Fred, you mentioned that uh the research on difference between face-
to-face and {situation X type of interaction} is somewhat contradictory. I won-
der if you have uh, well I put it, could you point to an example of a particular
point on which research, uh, it sort of seems to conflict? And uh, if you have
thought at all about why, why it may seem to conflict? Or uh, if there's any
explanation for why the research seems to be conflicting.

In formulating his question to Fred this way, the faculty member does
considerable work to make it okay for Fred not to have a very well-
thought-out answer. Rather than straightforwardly asking for Fred to give
an example, the faculty member asks him to "point to" one. The pointing formulation makes reasonable more vague, less detailed information
than if a person was asked to "give" an example. Moreover, the example
"pointed to," need illustrate no more than research that "sort of seems to
conflict." In addition, in asking for an explanation of the conflict he
explicitly recognizes that Fred may not have previously thought about
this ("if you have thought at all"). Thus, this question formulation does
a lot of work to make it "okay" for the student responder not to have a
good answer. The sheer amount of conversational work, in fact, calls
attention to itself. Why, we might ask, is this faculty member doing so
much work? To presume that a presenter would have difficulty giving an
example of his central claim is not an identity-neutral action. This is a
competency to be expected of all community members, including the
most novice. Thus, while it seems plausible that the faculty member was
working to avoid putting Fred on the spot, the amount of conversational
work done to make reasonable an inadequate answer implicitly conveys
to all who are present that a negative intellectual assessment is being
made of Fred by the question-poser. Similar to Ed's situation (Excerpt
41), the situated assessment of Fred's knowledgeability will depend on
his response. If rather than haltingly try to come up with an example,
which is what Fred did, he had challenged the implication—"Of course
I can supply an example, why wouldn't I? One place the research conflicts is . . .,"—then Fred could have overturned the faculty member's
implication that he had limited knowledge of something the community
expected him to know.

In sum, through the presence or absence of knowledgeability-limitation
markers, question formulations imply whether the recipient is expected to
know a particular piece of information. In conjunction with community
beliefs about the requested information and the recipient's actual
response, knowledgeability-limitation markers shape whether the question-recipient is seen to be appropriately knowledgeable. While this aspect
of identity work is most visible when question-posers repair their question

formulation or a mismatch occurs between projected and actual knowledge levels, it is routinely available in question formulations.

INTELLECTUAL ORIGINALITY, TIME REFERENCES, AND INTEREST QUERIES

When novice researchers are taught how to do scholarly work, the task is typically conceived as one of helping students master technical skills and discipline-bound argumentative conventions. That an academic can routinely make reasonable claims that are well supported with evidence is a sought-after intellectual identity. This aspect of competence is only part of what most academics seek; they also wish to be seen as doing interesting, novel work. Academics desire to be judged original thinkers. Kaufer and Geisler (1989) argue that for an idea to be labeled as new it must show its ties to earlier ideas while displaying that the introduced idea is more than a tired repetition of what others, including self, have said before.

Within this framework, a failure to tie to past work evidences inappropriate knowledgeability. Originality assessments will be more strongly tied to an academic's ability to say something new. In addition, besides being new, an original idea must be interesting (Davis, 1971)—it must elicit an increased attentiveness from people.

In this kind of discussion forum, challenges to a presenter's originality were made in two ways. One way was to link a presenter's topic to other work done in a non-present time frame and either directly state or imply the similarity of the two kinds of work. The other was to directly query whether what a person is doing is interesting or, through language loading, to imply that it is not.

Questions that directly described another as doing no more than what had been done in the past were not common but could be found. Consider the following question put by a faculty member to a graduate student:

Excerpt 43

I noticed that most of the literature you review is from the eighties ((Presenter: uh huh)) and some of it goes back to the seventies but nothing goes back to the ancient period of the fifties ((group laughter)) . . . *Didn't we have a human relations model back in the fifties? . . . Well what's new here since Roethlisberger and Rogers? What's new in the way of these variables? We're hearing the same stuff.*

In Excerpt 43, the faculty member not only directly and straightforwardly asks if there is anything new in what is being said ("What's new in the way of these variables?") but goes on to label explicitly what the student is presenting as "the same old stuff." In tying the student's topic to the past in this manner, this faculty member conveys a strong assessment of the student's work (and hence the student) as unoriginal.

While Excerpt 43 is the only instance in the discussion discourse of an originality challenge made so directly, the academic interviews at University X attest to their presence as well as memorability. Faculty member Joan recounted this kind of identity challenge in her graduate school colloquia experiences.

Excerpt 44

It wasn't just that it was heated debate . . . it was that, uh personal affront was intended and was taken in the course of, of this discussion. And perverse human that I am, I liked it . . . I loved seeing mild-mannered people sort of take incredible barbs and uh, digs at one another and people who had to work together forevermore, uh say things like, uh *"How's this different from your dissertation twenty years ago?"*

While originality often may not be challenged directly, it is there as an ongoing interactional sensitivity. Consider what is implied in the following comment-question made by a nondepartmental faculty member (Roger) in the opening questioning of a Ph.D. dissertation defense.

Excerpt 45

There's really a lot of interesting things I'd like to talk about and I have to be strategic because I know that other people have a lot of the same questions. Um, I really liked reading it. It's really well written. It's really fascinating. I, I um, it gets me back into traditional sociology too, which I haven't done for a while. And it was so much fun to read *and realize that people continue to find this stuff interesting.* Um, I guess the first thing is, starting at a grand theoretical level, um it seemed to me that, you know I don't read in discourse analysis per se. You know well *I was trying to get a grasp on what's the really interesting question?* What's the contribution here, you know? And it seemed that here, the one thing that you said was that developing a notion that {concept X's} occur . . . *I guess it reminded me very much of when we used to read and always criticize Parsons, when I was first a graduate student,* the notion, you know that people are somewhat captured by their roles . . . [345 more words]. And so I see kind of, two general, not clearly related theoretical questions. And I just wanted you to comment on to what extent you're about those things.

Following his explicitly face-supportive comments (e.g., "It's well written. It's really fascinating"), Roger goes on to make a lengthy comment-question, the thrust of which is to ask the student to disambiguate between two potentially contradictory claims in the study. As such, the question primarily challenges the student's argumentative skillfulness.

Embedded in this challenge, however, is an oblique challenge to the student's originality. Roger's question formulation challenges the student's originality in two ways. The first is expressed in time references embedded in this question. By characterizing the central issue in the student's work as one that occupied scholars more than a decade ago ("people continue to find this stuff interesting" and "it reminded me very much . . . of when I was first a graduate student"), Roger conveys that he sees the project as "dated" and doing no more than what has been done before.

Roger also challenges the intellectual originality of the work (and the student) by marking as problematic the task of figuring out what is newsworthy and interesting. In describing himself as "trying to get a grasp on what's the really interesting question," Roger implies that figuring out what's interesting takes considerable work. Although he specifically mentions a reason that would account for the difficulty as potentially his fault ("I don't read in discourse analysis per se"), given his considerably higher levels of experience/status and the implicit structure of the utterance—a pro forma disclaimer (I don't read in X but it doesn't seem interesting)—we are led to see it as a politeness move to soften a challenge rather than an account he is offering for a problem he has.

In Excerpt 46, we see both a time linkage and an interest query challenge made. In contrast to Excerpt 45, however, rather than directly questioning how someone's work is interesting, the question-poser characterizes the recipient's work with language implying that the work is dull, plodding and boring. In addition, the time linkage made is to the future rather than the past. Consider how these two moves operate together to challenge the presenter's originality.

Excerpt 46

Jim: I have one more question. It really strikes for me at the heart of the whole methodological question we've been talking about.

Jill: Uh huh.

Jim: One scenario would be for you to spend the next twenty years of your life uh doing replications with similar stimulus materials but methodological variations. Like you could do MDS [multidimensional scaling], you could do videotape, you could, if you wanta make sure you had similar stimulus materials because otherwise we might worry about whether or not you had comparability of results. And so uh, the strategy then would be a sort of piling on, an accumulation, bit by bit until

finally you were satisfied twenty years later that you were able
to say what was going on in this study of {X}. And uh, then
another approach might be to uh, go for something much
more dramatic and I'm not quite sure what that would be. It
would be the kind of thing where we could all say YES, for sure,
that's it, no question about it. Uh, as a philosophy of science is
this accumulated approach one that you can justify in light of
work in social psychology or communication, interpersonal
communication?

Consider the "choice" Jim offers Jill regarding her future twenty years
of research. She can either continue what she is doing, extending her findings step by step. To do this is to engage in "piling on" and "bit by bit accumulation." Or she could decide to do something "where we could all say
YES, for sure, that's it, no question about it." Jim's language is loaded with
negative evaluation toward where Jill seems to be going, and positive evaluation toward what is labeled as the alternative possible path. His language
implies that Jill's intended path is boring, pedestrian, and insignificant,
whereas the other is exciting, interesting, and valuable.

In addition, consider how Jim characterizes the net results of Jill's intellectual work in the future ("spend the next twenty years of your life uh
doing replications with similar stimulus materials but methodological
variations"). Such a characterization creates a vivid picture of Jill doing
virtually the same thing (not anything "new") for a long time.
Furthermore, in using "twenty years" as his future reference, Jim uses a
unit of time that has particular cultural meaning. "Twenty years," I suggest, is a specific time unit used to reference a person's life work; it is a
time marker that calls up assessment of the significance and value of what
a person has been doing (or is planning to do). Because all actions occur
in time, and are expected to take particular amounts of time, references
to time can become implicit ways to criticize (or praise) another's decisions, and projected actions. Thus, Jim's reference to "twenty years"
implies a negative assessment of Jill's potential originality if she continues
on her current trajectory. In sum, through linkages to time, as well as
queries about a work's interest value, question posers can raise challenges
to recipients' intellectual originality.

INTELLECTUAL SOPHISTICATION AND FRAMEWORK
PROBLEMATIZING THROUGH LEXICAL CHOICES

In addition to knowledgeability and originality, the activity of questioning
can challenge a recipient's level of intellectual sophistication. "Intellectual

sophistication" is an attribution made to academics who display the ability in their talk (or writing) to recognize the intellectual tradition within which they work, to grant its limitations while articulating its advantages, and to reveal awareness of what is entailed by and inconsistent with their framework.

That ideas are situated within intellectual traditions and involve particular assumptive frameworks I take to be a belief so widely shared that it requires no defense. Theoretical traditions—what I label intellectual frameworks—include epistemological and methodological commitments as well as knowledge of particular authors regarded as seminal. Differences in frameworks are especially notable across disciplinary boundaries (Bazerman, 1988; Tracy, 1988), but they exist within most scholarly communities.

Theoretical frameworks are called up in the way scholars talk about their own research and question others about theirs. Each intellectual tradition uses a vocabulary of central terms. To the initiated, these terms serve as cues to a speaker's intellectual framework. Just as an experienced sailor can recognize a large underwater iceberg from a small piece of ice in the ocean, so too can lexical choices cue intellectual traditions. For example, among language and social interaction scholars, talk about the "accomplishment of everyday experience" cues ethnomethodology (Garfinkel, 1967); references to "speech communities" and "speech events" cue the ethnography of communication (Hymes, 1974); mention of "experimental control" and "manipulation check" cue an experimental paradigm. Thus, in issuing a question, a speaker dons the cloak of an intellectual tradition.

When question formulations operate within the tradition of the question-recipient, the intellectual framework is backgrounded; assumptions remain implicit, unspoken, tacit. The discussion goes forward focusing on the substantive thrust of the question. When a questioner's lexical choices highlight or problematize the *framework as a framework*, however, a question-recipient needs to explicate and justify the assumptions of the framework. At such a juncture, the issue of the choice of that particular framework versus some other becomes salient. If a question-recipient does not recognize that a framework challenge has been issued, or inadequately defends his or her choice, the person displays self as having limited ability to move among intellectual worlds; in other words, the person displays a lack of intellectual sophistication. Consider, now, how this process works.

In Excerpt 47, Lee (a graduate student) asks Beth (an academic interviewing for an assistant professor position) about several specific choices she made. In her presentation, Beth had described an experimental study in which participants were presented with written conversational materials and were asked to make judgments about what a party said.

Excerpt 47

Lee: Okay so there was one example of a {X} message if they were to get one at all?

Beth: There were three examples. There was one example of [X] in the high/low, one in the low/high and one example in the low/low . . . [33 more words]

Lee: Yeah I got that. Now was the particular {X} message of the same sort?

Beth: Not, not all. Those that varied across conversation so the {X} example from the Jane and Sue conversation might have been different from the {X} example in the Jim and Todd situation.

Lee: Do you think that would have caused any kind of differences?

Beth: Is the question as to whether the differences in the {X} strategy might have? It's also possible the differences in the situation might have.

Lee: So you don't, you can't really tell?

In this sequence, Lee's questions convey concerns about Beth's experimental choices. They do not, however, problematize Beth's starting framework. In exploring whether variation in the study's outcomes can be attributed to other factors than the ones manipulated, Lee participates in an experimental framework. In so doing, she tacitly supports Beth's starting assumptions. Contrast Lee's questions of Beth with those from faculty member Sam at a slightly later point in the same discussion.

Excerpt 48

Sam: Did you have any dilemmas of choice in terms of experimentation here? Did you, did you *sacrifice* uh uh external validity for *control* at any point?

Beth: Uh yeah the, well I, our readings, I mean when they, when they read the conversations or read the scenarios that, yeah that *sacrifices* external validity for the purpose of *control* and what I was interested in controlling were things like information and uh, that kind of thing, so yeah.

Sam: So how far would you be willing to generalize this in light of the *sacrificing* that you did do?

In his questioning, Sam, like Lee, asks Beth to reflect on her choice-making as a researcher. In contrast, however, Sam's lexical choices gently flag Beth's intellectual framework as problematic. Evidence that Sam is querying the framework (experimental research) rather than operating within it is twofold.

First, his initial formulation asks about categories of action ("dilemmas of choice in terms of experimentation") rather than any specific choice Beth made in the experimental study she is discussing. Not focusing on a particular conveys that the issue is bigger or more basic than the specific choice, a move that goes with framework challenges.

Second, the reformulation of his question, made in the same initial utterance, replaces a relatively neutral phrase ("dilemmas of choice") with a formulation that carries negative evaluation of the experimental frame ("sacrificing external validity for control"). Among social scientists an accepted belief, well-documented in introductory research methods textbooks (e.g., Anderson, 1987; Bowers & Courtright, 1984) is that a good study must attend to multiple criteria that often are at odds with each other. Good research is expected to maximize both internal and external validity, but while good research attends to both, different traditions prioritize criteria differently. Thus it is generally accepted that good experiments satisfy internal validity better than other methods but do less well on external validity.

In asking Beth if she "sacrificed" something, Sam suggests that she has gone too far in the process of weighing competing criteria. Note, too, that Sam's question implies the direction in which Beth has gone too far. She sacrificed "external validity," the criterion nonexperimental traditions most often accuse experimental work of inadequately considering. Moreover, in using the term *control* rather than *internal validity*, Sam further tilts the comparison. Beth's decision is not cast as one between equally desirable goods (internal and external validity) but between a good (external validity) and the negative consequences of the means (control) used to achieve the other good (internal validity). *Control* as a lexical choice highlights that she has opted for contrivance and a lack of naturalness. Through this cooccurring set of lexical choices Sam problematizes Beth's starting framework.[3]

Does Beth recognize this simple question as a framework challenge and hence a bid to display her intellectual sophistication? I think she does, although she is unable to address it well. That Beth is aware of a challenge is suggested by the high level of nonfluency in her answering comment.

[3.] Judgments that lexical choices are intended by a speaker to problematize a framework are undoubtedly easier to make the better one knows a question poser's intellectual frame. When a questioner's starting framework is known to be different from the one a presenter takes, framework challenges are especially likely. In such a situation, wording choices that are negative in very subtle ways will often be taken as (and intended as) challenges. Sam had frequently expressed criticism of experimental research; for this reason I judge it highly unlikely that discussants who knew Sam well did not hear Sam's question as a framework challenge.

Her answer begins in four different ways ("uh yeah the," "well I," "our readings," "I mean when they") before she proceeds fluently. False starts give us information about the level of difficulty a speaker perceives in a question. Beth's unusually high number of false starts implies that she has recognized a difficulty.

The substance of her response, however, does not address the framework challenge. Her response, in fact, buys into Sam's negative characterization ("yeah that sacrifices external validity for the purpose of control"). To display herself as intellectually sophisticated, I would suggest, Beth needed to acknowledge her commitment to an experimental research tradition while arguing for its value compared to other approaches. To do this Beth needed to call into question what was presupposed by Sam's use of the word *sacrifice* as well as to reframe her tradition using positively loaded language. For instance, if Beth had said, "I wouldn't use the word sacrifice. All research involves trade-offs between internal and external validity. My research is experimental and as such has stronger commitments to internal validity than more anecdotal approaches do," she would have displayed a higher level of intellectual sophistication than she did, and would have accused the other tradition of being merely anecdotal.

Besides implicitly criticizing an intellectual framework, a questioner's lexical choices can problematize whether a presenter is operating within the intellectual framework he or she has claimed. Excerpt 49 is from an all-day professional seminar among a group of established scholars who share an ethnographically based intellectual frame. In his presentation, Larry has criticized the "flecks of positivism allegiances" evident in the work of others present at the seminar. In response to a first question, Larry argues that his interpretive approach to knowledge is better than the traditional positivistic ones. He characterizes the positivistic tradition with negatively loaded language ("its very susceptible to being aligned with hegemonic forces, colonization and so forth") and describes his stance positively (his stance is "performative, processual, open, open to new insights, more voices, particularly minority voices can join the conversation"). Following this response, Thomas, another seminar participant, does a semantic analysis:

Excerpt 49

Tom: As I listen to your answer to the question, I'm tempted to turn the tables on you some, particularly in terms of your language which I might turn around and talk about the arrogance of nonpositivism ((short simultaneous talk)) the use of the word contradictions, the use of the word polemic, ((L: is loaded)), suggest to me an either/or. And it seems to me particularly as I hear your earlier comment about pluralism, your comment now in reference to this question, that the real position is not either/or, it's both/and.

Larry: Yeah I, no quarrel there. And you are right to chasten me if anything that I said seems not to be embracing pluralism. You know I argue, I certainly argue with the positivists. But as I said earlier, not to displace that, not, to engage in a conversation. Now I'm committed not only to cultural pluralism but to methodological pluralism.

Tom's comment/question characterizes Larry as speaking in ways that are inconsistent with his intellectual framework. Tom's comment suggests that an intellectual committed to pluralism would see value in many different perspectives and would not talk in disparaging or dismissive ways about views different from his own. In choosing the word arrogant, Larry implicitly accuses him of talking in a manner inconsistent with commitments of his intellectual frame.

Larry's response recognizes the validity of the framework challenge and seeks to address it. By making explicit the interactive thrust of Tom's comment as well as the reasoning on which it rested ("no quarrel there . . . you are right to chasten me if anything I said seems not to embrace pluralism"), Larry shows recognition of an entailment of his intellectual framework. At the same time he works to reframe the meaning of his conversational behavior (he's arguing with the positivists to engage in conversation, not to put them down). In recognizing and granting the legitimacy of an entailment while showing how his actions should not be read as inconsistent with it, Larry displays high intellectual sophistication.

In sum, how intellectually sophisticated an academic is becomes salient when a question problematizes the person's intellectual framework. Such problematizing is accomplished through subtle lexical choices. That is, particular linguistic formulations cue intellectual traditions and in so doing may unveil what is typically tacit and hidden—that presenters' ideas are sensible only within particular assumptive structures. Relatedly, specific formulations can make visible a questioner's doubts about a tradition, or doubts that a person is operating within a claimed tradition. Thus, when a questioner's lexical choices make the presenter's framework problematic, the presenter's intellectual sophistication is challenged. Of note is the fact that the challenge can end up supporting the person's intellectual sophistication, as was seen with Larry, or can reveal its relative absence, as seen with Beth.[4]

[4.] It is to be expected that graduate students will display lower levels of intellectual sophistication than more experienced academics. This is because intellectual sophistication is developed by a person participating in discussion communities where framework challenges occur. For many academics this kind of challenge does not occur until they take academic positions in institutions different from those in which they were trained.

5

Character Challenges

In traditional treatises on argument, challenges to positions that focus on the personal character of the speaker are labeled "ad hominem fallacies."[1] Within this conception of good argument, to attack or criticize the person who is advocating an idea, rather than to focus on the idea itself, is an illegitimate kind of argument. A difficulty with this conception is its presumption that ideas and people are easily separable. People are personally and politically implicated in the ideas they pursue—and they should be. Just as the pursuit of a particular research issue cues whether one is a relatively theoretical or practical intellectual, so too do the selection and framing of an issue convey information about a person's broader values and character.

That character and information are inescapably connected has been most vividly documented in studies of the courtroom. Penman (1987, 1990, 1991) shows that courtroom rules are designed to insure that information-getting (displaying) remains the central function of talk in the courtroom. Yet while getting to the truth may be the focal language game, there is an equally important identity game occurring simultaneously. In particular, attorneys are using their questions to draw moral pictures of

---

[1] Introductory texts used in college courses to teach argumentation and critical thinking often present all personal character arguments as inappropriate. For instance, in their discussion of ad hominem argument, Browne and Keeley say this: "One does not prove a point by attacking the person. The assumption that because a person may have undesirable qualities, his ideas are therefore undesirable is clearly a bad assumption. Such an argument diverts attention from the issue. A good argument attacks ideas, not the person with the ideas. Attacking a person, rather than ideas is frequently called ad hominem argument" (1990, p. 121). As Walton (1989) shows in his study of political questioning, character arguments are warrantable under certain circumstances.

67

witnesses. Specific ways of formulating a question are used to imply that a witness is a reasonable, honest person on the one hand, or deceptive, sleazy, and untrustworthy on the other; that is, through the ways questions are formulated and sequenced (and witnesses answer them), a picture of the witness's character is offered to the judge or jury. Moreover, this is not merely an occasional by-product of talk that is unfortunate and to be ignored; juries are specifically instructed that the demeanor of witnesses—made visible through the talk exchanges—is relevant to assessment of the facts.

Woodbury (1984) illustrates in detail how attorneys draw upon the interactive presumptions entailed by the grammatical form of a question to build a positive or negative moral character for a witness. For instance, to ask a question in the negative ("You didn't go to the door?") conveys that the question-asker is surprised by what a person asserted. Surprise in everyday life is routinely exhibited when a person does not act in a way that is expected or reasonable. Thus, for a questioner to act surprised (which a negatively worded question conveys) can be used to portray a witness's action, and hence the witness, as unreasonable.

In intellectual discussion, issues of character usually are less salient than they are in the courtroom. No immediate decisions are being made that have consequence for people's material and reputational lives. Moreover, it is not unusual for academic discussion to be "academic" in the pejorative sense used by everyday speakers. That is, the topic's relevance for everyday life may not be at all evident. Other discussion topics, on the other hand, are what I would call "decision-making implicative." The topic, by virtue of its connection with institutions and practices in society, makes relevant questions about what ought to be. In these cases a scholar's personal and moral character becomes situationally relevant. In decision-implicative discussions, issues of whose material interests will be served and whether what is being proposed is ethically defensible become relevant. The raising of these issues in the context of a scholar's specific project cannot be other than a character challenge.[2] Raising the issue of interests carries an implication that an academic may be serving the interests of social groups whose interests should not be served; similarly, raising issues of morality implies that something unethical is being advocated.

[2.] When these comments are raised in a broad and abstract way about entire lines of research, or typical disciplinary efforts, the central thrust of such comments is to challenge the intellectual sophistication of a presenter. That is, does a scholar recognize that research frames entail assumptions about the knowledge-generation process, either that knowledge generation is thought of as a relatively objective process or that it is conceived as a socially positioned act? When the issue of interests comes up at the level of an individual scholar's work, however, the challenge becomes a personal one.

In the next sections, some different ways that the issue of material interests was raised at State U are illustrated. The seriousness of such challenges is shown to be affected by presenters' positions in relation to their ideas, these places are constructed through the discursive moves of questioners and presenters. Then, a disagreement between two faculty members about how political campaigning should be conducted is analyzed to show how a disputing party can often reframe a challenge to his or her ethicality as evidence of the other's naïveté.

WHOSE INTERESTS ARE BEING SERVED?

Raising the issue of interests challenges the integrity of a presenter, but whether the query is meant (and taken) as a serious challenge or a relatively minor one depends on how closely the presenter has aligned with the ideas about which he or she is talking. Consider the differences displayed in Excerpts 50 and 51. Excerpt 50 is from the discussion following a presentation by a graduate student, Elise. Elise had made a presentation overviewing past research on motivation in the workplace and in her talk identified communication strategies that managers use to motivate employees. Well into the discussion period a faculty member, Walt, pursued an issue he had raised earlier.

Excerpt 50

Walt: Well no . . . it really goes back to my question about human resources. A distinction you applied before that I found mind boggling between strategic use of management and human resources use of management. (E: uhm hmm) When all I'm hearing is, in talking about human resources is, strategies for getting people to see the goals of the organization as desirable because it's seen that, look what the Japanese do when they see that, they'll work harder *but I'm not hearing anywhere in there anything about those organizational goals having anything to do with the goals of people who work for the company.* Uh and where that's coming from, in any way interact with that

Elise: Well, I think you have to make the assumption of ethics and integrity. And I, I suppose probably ((chuckle)) that's pretty wild.

Rom: You do? ((loud group laughter))

Elise: *Uhm I mean I would argue that it needs to be* part of it, yeah but that there needs to be a real attempt to look at whether or not the employee in back wants to have an enriched job and would benefit from that. But I said earlier I think there's all kinds of people out there that, that's not their concern at all. And so I don't see why it should be the concern, the total concern of the manager, I think it's just, as I see it, a repertoire of skills.

Walt: It's a, it's a repertoire of appearances. It's not just ( ). Does the organization really care about that person?

Of note are the ways Walt's comments strongly imply that Elise's work is serving the interests of people in power and failing to take account of interests of regular working people. In saying "All I'm hearing is X but I'm not hearing Y," Walt implies the moral rightness of Y. Furthermore, when Walt counters Elise's characterization ("a repertoire of skills") with ("a repertoire of appearances") his wording sets up a sense of the communicative activity Elise advocates as shallow and manipulative rather than one of professional skill.

Elise defends her position with a "yes but" utterance (Yes, ethics are important, but not all employees want "enriched" jobs). Her remarks, however, position her at some distance from the ideas she is talking about. In starting her rejoinder with "Uhm I mean I would argue that" rather than immediately beginning with the substance of her disagreement, she conveys herself as overlooking rather than directly involved in the disagreement. Her own wording, in line with her institutional status (graduate student) and her project (largely reviewing the work of prior research) minimizes the severity of challenge; that is, the personal import for Elise of this research being accused of serving the powers that be is minimized because of her distance from the research. Compare this exchange with one that occurred between two faculty members in Excerpt 51.

Len has presented the outlines of a major research project about religion that had been funded by an outside granting agency. In the opening of his talk, Len positioned himself very close to the ideas about which he was talking—he has thought about the larger set of issues for a long time, he has written a book, and he has received grants.

Excerpt 51

Sid: Uhm, actually that answer was kind of getting into the area that I wanted to explore and that has to do with uh, well one way to put it would be how, *how does this research sort of situate itself in relation to the play of interests involved here.* Uh whose interest is this serving is kind of a crude way of putting it. Uh well maybe that's a good place to start.

Len: Okay, sure even I, I think that's a, that's a, uh one of the first uh questions that came to mind when I considered doing it. Um let me say one thing parenthetically before I begin on that. I think in general I find studying religion is troublesome for that reason. Now people assume you have an agenda either positive or negative when you look at religion that may not go along when you're studying pornography. Uhm and so you know that's an, that's an assumption that sort of overarches all the others. Now the specifics of this study . . .

In contrast to Walt's comment to Elise, which characterizes her research as inappropriately serving management rather than worker interests, Sid raises the issue of interests more neutrally. His direct question does not imply that Len's research is serving inappropriate interests, but it does flag it as an issue for which a good answer is expected. Of interest is the way Len's response displays his acceptance of a responsibility he has as a researcher. His response shows that he sees ideas, societal interests, and self's actions as tied. In saying "that's a, uh one of the uh questions that came to mind when I considered doing it," Len displays that he sees research as an activity that is not neutral and apolitical; he affirms the reasonableness of links between his character and his research pursuits. At the same time, though, he works to mitigate the intensity of the connection by suggesting that higher standards of moral accountability are invoked in studies of religion in contrast to other equally sensitive areas of research.

In certain ways, Walt's comment to Elise can be seen as more challenging than Sid's question to Len. The comment directed toward Elise had a strong accusatory flavor absent from Sid's "information question," yet Len's response indicated that he interpreted the question as more of a character challenge than was seen with Elise. That a speaker's positioning in relation to ideas is a central contributor to challenge seriousness is further suggested by Excerpt 51, a continuation of Elise's discussion. Consider the comment a faculty member, Renee, makes to Elise.

Excerpt 52

Renee: Does org comm [organizational communication], or let me state a bias up front and then you can address it. It seems to me, my biggest criticism of uh much, much of the study in organizations is that it takes the place to focus, it takes the structure of organizations as a given and says within that

structure that assumes these goals and this is what's important, how do you maximize with the whole set of assumptions staying the same? So you're not asking how you
restructure, what, you're not changing the output. You can
vary within a very narrow range. What can a manager do
differently uh that will affect things but you don't think of
restructuring the way people talk to each other or the way
jobs are divided or how employees can influence managers
to bring about changes in the organization that would
make it, it a better workplace on some other dimension
than short-term cash flow or even long-term cash flow or
whatever it might be.

Renee begins her comment as a question and then repairs it to make it
a statement about which she asks for comment. The primary implication
that changes when Renee changes from a question to a comment is the
degree of responsibility attributed to Elise for the ideas being discussed. In
the initial question formulation "Does org comm", the formulation presupposes that Elise is a suitable representative of organizational communication and can be asked to speak for the research enterprise. That is, the
initial formulation casts Elise as in the center of the tradition, positioned
closely to the ideas. In changing the question to a comment, Renee makes
Elise's relation to these ideas more ambiguous and leaves them unspeci-
fied. She is not held directly responsible for what the research tradition
has done. In that sense, Elise can, if she chooses, hear Renee's comment
as a complaint about a research tradition rather than as a criticism of her
own intellectual choices.

Renee's repair further suggests that intellectual positioning is not a one-
time activity done by speakers in the beginning of their talk. Rather, it is an
ongoing activity carried out by questioners and presenters to serve their
immediate discussion needs. Whether Renee's motive in softening the
challenge was out of concern for Elise, to lessen the possibility of appearing self-aggrandizing herself, or both, is unclear. Regardless of Renee's
motive, her comment gives evidence that the severity of character challenges can be influenced by the distance a comment imputes a presenter
to be from the ideas.

REFRAMING: UNETHICAL OR NAÏVE?

When presentation topics are decision-implicative, they implicitly propose
what should or should not be done. In such cases, morality and practical
feasibility are two criteria that become salient. These criteria often pull in

different directions. A proposal that claims to be morally right, can often be reframed as practically problematic. An example of this pattern is displayed in an exchange between faculty members Jerry and Paul.

Following Bush's election in 1988, Jerry made a presentation analyzing the U.S. presidential campaign strategies of George Bush and Michael Dukakis. In his presentation, Jerry reported that he had predicted Dukakis would lose the election at that point in the campaign where Dukakis had a significant lead in the polls. Toward the end of his presentation, Jerry recounted an argument he and Paul had previously had about suitable next moves for the Democratic party. Several minutes into the discussion, Paul launches into a lengthy comment/question.

Excerpt 53

Paul: Uh first, uh right before you told the story about, when you told the story about, when you told me that what I was saying was bullshit because I said that we should, that they should explain what liberalism is. You said that Dukakis at the beginning of the campaign should have said, "I'm a liberal and this is why I'm a liberal and this is why I'm a great liberal." So I'm not sure

Jerry: in 30 seconds

((*group laughter*))

Paul: Oh, so it's the length. Uh at the beginning of uh, uh your talk, you said that you were kinda torn between, well either we should play ( ) and play it clean, um and be horrible. Or we should decide that winning is really important and so we'll do anything that's necessary to win, which to me seems like a false dichotomy. It suggests that you can't play clean without being stupid. Uh and what I noticed in your talk is that you shifted back and forth between bemoaning the sorry state of campaigning, bemoaning the ethics of it, bemoaning the fact that decisions are made based on virtually nothing. Uhm and then talking about well this tactic would work and that tactic would work. So it was kinda, you were shifting back either to an ethical perspective, talking about how bad things were to, to a purely tactical perspective, saying this would work and that would work and the other would work. And I was wondering if you say anyway that you might be able to combine those two, so that you could use tactics that might be effective but

	that also might be ethical and maybe help make the campaign more ethical?
Jerry:	Well sure whenever you can, be ethical and effective uh
((*group laughter*))	
Jerry:	and when you can't be then=
Audience:	[=be effective
	[=look effective
Jerry:	look for different ways of being effective . . .

Paul's opening remarks reference Jerry's earlier comment about what he had said ("what I was saying was bullshit"). Of note is the fact that Paul uses more negative language to portray Jerry's characterization of his position ("bullshit") than Jerry himself used. Paul then goes on to suggest that Jerry made a point in his presentation that was identical to the one Paul had made earlier. Jerry's response, "in 30 seconds," acknowledges the legitimacy of Paul's earlier comment but minimizes its importance. In naming such a short amount of time (thirty seconds) to make the kind of point that Paul is advocating Dukakis should have done, Jerry is minimizing the amount of agreement he has with Paul's proposal.

Paul continues to try to formulate what is wrong with Jerry's position. Paul first accuses Jerry of making a "false dichotomy." Somewhat later he accuses him of inconsistency—shifting between two perspectives. Both comments challenge Jerry intellectually: Can Jerry show his position to be argumentatively coherent? Simultaneously embedded in this utterance, however, is a subtle character challenge.

That Paul is questioning Jerry's character is implied through several discourse moves. First, the sequencing of Paul's contrasts shows a patterned order. Paul twice describes Jerry as mentioning the ethical and then dropping it for the tactical ("bemoaning the ethics of it . . . and then talking about how well this tactic would work," "shifting back either to an ethical perspective . . . to a purely tactical perspective"). Paul's final question asks Jerry whether the ethical can be combined with the effective; but given Paul's prior ordering of the two concerns, an implicit accusation stands that Jerry has given too much attention to the tactical and inadequate attention to the ethical. That this comment is a character challenge is further suggested by the conversational mitigation work that Paul does in producing it. Mitigation is visible in the prefacing "And I was wondering," the hypothetical situation framing "if you would say," and the muted amount of commitment called for ("might use tactics" versus "would"). While the mitigation softens the challenge, it does not eliminate it. In implying that the proposal Jerry is advocating is unethical, Paul implies that Jerry himself is unethical.

Jerry's response does not address Paul's intellectual challenge (false dichotomy? inconsistency?); nor does it directly speak to the implicit moral challenge (advocating the unethical?). Rather, Jerry seeks to reframe the character issue as one of Paul's naïveté. Jerry reframes the character issue through his overly quick agreement: "Well sure." While agreeing with Paul at a superficial level, Jerry can be seen as disagreeing at a deeper level. In saying "Well sure" Jerry portrays Paul's position as idealistic and unworldly (who would say otherwise in this clear easy case?). Implied by Jerry's quick agreement is the easiness, and hence atypicality, of this case. Jerry suggests the unwordliness of Paul's position through his use of a cultural cliché (if you can't be both X and Y, be Y) which the group participates in completing. In essence the quick agreement casts Paul as naïve, a person failing to recognize the complexities and tensions of the everyday world.

In sum, challenges to an academic's character can arise whenever the ideas being discussed have planning and decision-making consequences. On such occasions, presenters are held morally accountable for what they advocate. Questions about the morality or practicality of a proposal, or about the material interests served by a particular set of ideas cannot escape being challenges to the character of the person.

So far we have viewed the problems of the departmental colloquium through presenters' and discussants' eyes. From this vantage point, with our dilemmatic lens in place, we have been able to make sense of apparently off-the-cuff comments, question wording and rewording, disclaimers and accounts, and situational framing work. In the next section, different dilemmas and discourse practices become visible as the situation is viewed from the group perspective.

II

Dilemmas of the Group

6

Equality and Expertise

An egalitarian pattern within an inegalitarian social structure is fraught with dilemmatic aspects (p. 66).

It is precisely those whose expertise is deemed unequal who must be reassured that personally they are just as valuable as anyone else (p. 75).

These quotes come from a discussion about the dilemma of equality/expertise that Billig and his colleagues (1988) see as deeply embedded in Western democratic societies. As an ideology, democracy is committed to the value of hearing all voices in a controversy; each person's opinion is to be respected and treated equally. At the same time, most contemporary democratic societies are structured around elaborate credentialing systems in which sets of individuals (authorities) determine whether other individuals possess sufficient knowledge to be legitimated as experts. Within these credentialing systems, experts become people who have earned the right to have their opinion privileged. Thus, in U.S. society there is an ideological dilemma: Both equality and expertise are valued, but each is at odds with the other.

In this chapter, I explore how the equality-expertise dilemma gets played out in academic discussion. In examining this issue, we take a step back from the State U case and focus on interviews conducted at University X (see Appendix B). Drawing upon these interviews, I argue that the expertise-equality dilemma is expressed in academic colloquia in terms of two sets of tensions. The first set of tensions centered on the appropriate link between institutional rank and idea examination. Interviewees believed both that ideas should be examined in light of intrinsic merit (ignore the rank of presenter), and that they should be examined in light of a presenter's experience level (attend to rank). The second set of tensions revolved around participation practices. Interviewees believed both that participation should be guided by a person's topic knowledgeability, and at the same time that all participants should speak up and be willing to risk themselves. First, a few comments about the discussion situation.

Habermas (1979) characterizes situations that bring about good discussion as those involving freedom from constraint. Such an ideal speech situation, he argued, can exist only when participants have equal opportunity to speak. In interviews, participants were specifically asked if they thought equality was necessary for good discussion. Consider how participants of different ranks responded.

Excerpt 54

The assumption that I was operating with was that in intellectual conversation you'll have *some semblance of equality.* (graduate student)

Excerpt 55

I think that people should be *somewhat equal* in terms of their interests, involvement, uhm again capability to engage in the discussion per se, to understand the ideas and to try to process them. And I think that's really important for it to work. (junior faculty member)

Excerpt 56

I think there is a need for people to presume that there is an *equalness of, of everybody's at least at a certain level of right to participate.* I don't think there's a need to presume that everybody's equally good, equally good in all things or that experience is equal. But there has to be some sense that we have the right to participate in this. (senior faculty member)

Like Habermas, interviewees believed that some type of rough equality or at least absence of marked inequality was necessary for good discussion, but participants in this academic institutional context were unequal in visible salient ways. As a graduate student remarked:

Excerpt 57

In colloquium it's not equal. There are people who are senior faculty and junior faculty and students, beginning graduate students.

How these rank differences did, or should, affect discussion was perceived differently by different participants. By and large it seemed that those of higher rank thought the advantages of rank could be minimized more easily than did those of lower rank. One faculty member noted, "We're in this big hierarchy and there are these status differences, but they can be minimized and down-played" (advanced junior faculty). That a person's institutional status might influence the salience of rank was explicitly acknowledged by one senior professor: "I'm sure it [equality] seems more possible to me than people who don't have tenure yet, that's my guess." Eleanor, a junior professor, argued that people in power frequently fail to recognize the advantages their position gives them. In support of her position she recounts the following story about the departmental colloquium:

Excerpt 58[1]

The full professor males used to talk 80% of the time. I mean, it just so happened that they were males. I guess gender didn't have anything to do with it because it was completely confounded. But they would talk all the time and the graduate students would almost never talk. And this came up as to how you get involved, how you get a turn in the conversation. And Ted [a senior male professor] said, "I was never able to get a turn in the conversation until I learned that I just had to start talking when somebody else was talking and then they would stop." Now he didn't realize first of all that's really rude. The other thing is I don't think he realized the extent to which his status bought him that. Whenever he wanted to interrupt he got to talk and the other person stopped talking. Whenever it got to a battle of the floor it was almost always equals who would battle it out and neither one would give in. And he and the others just presumed that they could talk as long as they wanted to and if somebody else was dying to get in it was by no means their obligation to let the people have the floor. So that was very striking I thought. And I became convinced from Ted that you just, especially from Ted, that you just kind of take those prerogatives for granted after a while. You have the power and you don't even realize that they're working for you. Like in that book *Parallel Lives* by Phyllis Rose, she talks about power in relationships. And she says it's like a tennis game where if the wind is blowing against you, you recognize that you have to fight against it. If it's blowing in your direction, then you just assume it's your backhand. You don't realize that the forces are all working in your favor. That's the way that went and it really disturbs me when graduate students don't either choose to talk or get a chance to talk, especially bad if they don't get a chance to talk, if they have to play by those rude and status-oriented rules.

[1.] This is the longest excerpt used from the interviews. To aid readability in this case, I have cleaned up the transcript by deleting false starts, repetitions, and most nonfluencies.

Eleanor's account vividly highlights the experience of lower institutional rank. From her point of view, lower status involves an ongoing awareness of the forces privileging high-status others and acting against self. Unsurprisingly, graduate students too experienced the rank differences as significant influences on their communicative behavior. Not only did graduate students see the opportunity to talk to be influenced by rank—as Eleanor identified—but they also saw the content of what could be expressed as shaped by their rank.

Excerpt 59

As a graduate student you think you can't say, well you really worry that you can't push something. Or you couldn't really press somebody. Or say I don't think, or you don't understand what I'm trying to do. That's off limits. It doesn't matter, you have to lead in to some sort of deference.

That inequality is an operative force in the discussion is implicitly supported by a comment from another graduate student. He responded to the interview question about the role of equality by saying:

Excerpt 60

I think equality is essential which is perhaps why they [faculty] *try to make* us [graduate students] feel like there is not very much hierarchy and so forth, what we say is significant, we don't have to take what they say as something being handed down to us.

In saying "they try to make us feel like there is not very much hierarchy" graduate student Ralph affirms rather than denies the influence of hierarchy. That is, speakers generally do not describe others as "trying" when they are successful. To say they tried is an implicit way to mark their lack of success while crediting the other with effort or good intentions.

In sum, the academic department is hierarchical—a context at odds with what people believe is necessary to create good discussion. In the above comments participants focused on the problematic side of power differences, highlighting advantages that accrue to those with more power. The situation is more complex than this, however. If unmerited power were the only problem, the solution would be relatively straightforward, though perhaps difficult to achieve: Power should be equalized.

Such a move, however, would destroy much of what is of value in academic institutions. The hierarchy in academic institutions reflects individual differences in experience and accomplishments; that is, those with more power and status (professors) are also the people who typically have more knowledge, experience, and skill than those with less status and power (students). Seen in this way, inequality is not only necessary, but a desirable feature of academic settings. This value of inequality is given attention by Lee, a junior faculty member.

Excerpt 61

I don't believe that graduate students are equal with faculty . . . if they were I think positions ought to be different. I really believe there is a reason for going to graduate school. So I'm, I don't believe in equality in that kind of sense.

In fact, participants faced a dilemma that most had not thought through in any explicit way. On the one hand, they recognized the importance of making distinctions among people in terms of expertise and knowledgeability. On the other, they believed in the need to respect each person as equal. This dilemma was at times reflected in some unusual, even contradictory formulations. In struggling to describe the relationship between faculty and graduate students, Lee describes faculty as "a little higher in the equal status kind of thing." Similarly, graduate student Jed answers a question about praise this way:

Excerpt 62

And praise I think is especially crucial for those of us who are *lower on the equality scale.*

These formulations are intriguing because they combine what would seem antithetical: Equality eschews rank distinctions; hierarchical relationships—being higher or lower—preclude equality. Why then did participants use this bizarre descriptor? Were they just confused and inarticulate? Probably not. Rather, the formulations capture in an especially vivid way the nature of faculty/graduate student relationships, a kind of relationship in which competing conceptions of the relationship are, and should be, taken seriously.

AN IDEA'S MERIT OR PRESENTER'S EXPERIENCE LEVEL?

The upshot of this is a problem. The nature of the institutional context does not match well the situational condition expected to facilitate good discussion. This mismatch leads to the first set of contradictory beliefs about communication. Participants thought they were expected to respond to ideas on their merit alone. At the same time, they thought they should take account of the experience level of the person to whom they were making a comment. Of interest is the fact that these different principles tended to surface in different relational contexts. When senior people made comments, participants felt it particularly important to examine an idea on its merit rather than attending to the status of the speaker.

Excerpt 63

I think it's desirable to try to look at everybody's idea from the point of view of the merits of the idea rather than who you think they are. (senior faculty member)

Excerpt 64

There's something about a kind of willingness to minimize as much as possible my claim on my ideas, my status as a person in, in its relation to the status of the ideas that I'm talking about and so forth [that makes for good intellectual discussion]. (senior faculty member)

In the above excerpts, the participants, both of whom are senior faculty, identify explicitly a desirable way to act: ideas should be examined on their merit. Each comment also implies what participants took to be a routine difficulty in intellectual discussion: ideas are given approval (or not seriously challenged) because a speaker possessed status. In essence, to combat a problem of ideas receiving unwarranted deference because of a speaker's high status, participants' solutions—their beliefs about a good way to talk—highlighted the importance of making status irrelevant to the examination of ideas. However, when the focus changed to novices or low-status participants, so too did participants' beliefs about good ways to talk.

Consider Rita's comment when she was asked about the kind of climate that best promotes intellectual discussion:

Excerpt 64

. . . a climate where everybody feels that they can say what they have to say and that they'll listened to, and that their, *uh ideas will be evaluated on their merit.* Uhm and that, oh this is important, a climate where people's idea and *contributions are evaluated according to where they are in the process* so that, at {Y University} where there were all these sorts of barracuda attacks on speakers, they were not, that never happened when it was a graduate student presenting. It happened in a much diluted, there I, I remember one person came for a job interview who was an assistant professor fresh out of school. That person was dealt with much more gently than someone who came to interview as an associate professor, somebody who was several years along. And uh later someone who had given a very pointed criticism said, "I feel those people have to take whatever comes." Uh but that was not the expectation of the junior faculty person. And it wasn't, never was the expectation of graduate students. (junior faculty member)

In the opening of her comment, Rita orients to the desirability of ideas being criticized on their merits. While she did not state this explicitly, her later comparison with graduate students suggests that her initial focus was upon faculty. When her attention shifts to lower status presenters, she contradicts herself, arguing for the need to be more gentle and considerate. In arguing that criticism of ideas should be couched in ways that recognize others' limited experiences, she is highlighting a problem in examining an idea on its own merit. In essence, if ideas are examined on their own merit, the most inexperienced and vulnerable members of the group (graduate students) are likely to receive stronger and more frequent criticism. Thus, a disjunction characterized the beliefs of most interviewees. In essence while participants expressed the belief that an idea should be considered on its own merit, participants also thought ideas should be examined in terms of a speaker's experience level.

Generally, participants believed that graduate students should be criticized more carefully and praised more fulsomely than was needed with faculty. That praise should be given more quickly to graduate students was an opinion voiced by a graduate student in Excerpt 62; it was also expressed by faculty members:

Excerpt 66

I think praise when it's honest should always be expressed. I don't think dishonest praise ever should be expressed. Uh, uh so I'm likely to say, *to especially a student* but also a colleague . . . if I think it's true, that I admire the work. (senior faculty member)

What, I would ask, is the significance of distinguishing between colleagues and students? If ideas are considered on their own merit, then why would one attend to the status of a speaker? Does the speaker believe a different standard should be used to assess the praiseworthiness of a student's

versus a colleague's idea? On the surface the comment suggests little conflict, but there must be. Given students' lower levels of knowledge and
experience, their ideas are less likely to be praiseworthy if assessed in terms
of an absolute standard of merit. This problem is acknowledged by a
senior professor.

Excerpt 67

There's a way in which in the classroom you say to someone "very good" and
um what you mean is very good for a student at this point in the course,
etcetera, etcetera, etcetera. Uh you know yesterday I was teaching my daughter how to ride a bicycle and if she got, if she made one turn of the pedals
without my grabbing the bike, you know that was great, right? But that does-
n't mean she's good at riding a bicycle. . . . You see to me intellectual discussion is a discussion, is a discussion that is in principle let's say among
equals uhm, and so there's a kind of praise which could be considered
patronizing uh, it's a kind of praise that is given by an authority to somebody
who is in a lower position.

Thus, if students are to be praised with any frequency at all, there must
be consideration of their experience level. This implies that what could
count as a good student idea will not necessarily count as a good faculty
idea. The problem, though, is that talking in this way not only reinforces
existing status differences, but increases them.

In sum, for faculty-student colloquia an important precondition for
good discussion is questionably present. Equality among participants is
needed for good discussion, yet participants are not equal. Thus we see the
first set of contrary beliefs: Participants in academic discussion are expected
to evaluate ideas on their own merit, and they are expected to evaluate
ideas in terms of the level of academic experience of the idea presenter.

Of interest is the fact that participants did not seem aware that they
believed contrary things. One explanation for this may be the different
words used to frame each belief. That is, when people framed what was disvalued, they tended to talk about "being influenced by status." In contrast,
when they talked positively about a person's status influencing participation, they were more likely to frame it as being sensitive to another's experience level. Obviously status and experience are highly connected, but
each points to a different evaluation about what is a suitable course of
action. As Billig (1987) notes, "phrases and single words can have definite
implications of accusation and justification. . . . The very use of one phrase
rather than another will, then, indicate the seed, if not the flower of an
argumentative position" (p. 207). Whether, and how, to take account of
status were not the only areas in which participants revealed contrary

beliefs: a second set of contrary beliefs surfaced regarding appropriate levels of participation.

KNOWLEDGEABILITY OR EQUAL WILLINGNESS TO RISK?

One question posed to participants was whether intellectual discussion occurred in the undergraduate classroom. Most interviewees felt that while it could, it generally did not occur. Consider what Sheryl, a junior faculty member, had to say in response to this question:

Excerpt 68

I think there is some intellectual discussion that occurs, and I think it's a little bit on the primitive side. And, I don't mean this nastily, well, I think in general when you're dealing with 18-, 19-, and 20-year-olds, they haven't done a lot of reading outside of what's been assigned and so bringing in information beyond their, to this point, very limited reading, very limited experience, you know their cloistered lives as examples. Um they haven't got any data to work with in the same level. So that, yeah, I think there's intellectual inquiry and intellectual discussion that goes on but I think it's pretty basic, you know, 'cause I just think you've gotta have read more and lived more and thought more before you can have real intellectual discussion.

Sheryl's explanation of why intellectual discussion is limited or "primitive" in the undergraduate classroom points to a constraint that comes into play in graduate settings as well. Good intellectual discussion requires a certain amount of knowledge and experience. Kris maintained that intellectual discussion happens "any time there are experts trying to make determination of a particular issue," and identified as characteristic of good discussion that

Excerpt 69

people would have sort of, the same level of interest in the topic being discussed or the same level of expertise in the areas being discussed. (junior faculty member)

Kris's comments highlight two features believed characteristic of good discussion: that people possess knowledge about an area, and that participants have roughly the same amount of it. As noted in the prior section, this second condition almost never exists in the graduate education setting. How much should people participate, though, if they do not know as much as other participants? One belief about what is appropriate is spelled out in a junior faculty member's comment:

Excerpt 70

I think that people who know the most and care the most about what's going on ought to be talking the most and the people who know less or care less, ought to talk less. (junior faculty member)

That participation should be guided by expertise level is not an unproblematic assertion, however. This is alluded to in another faculty member's comment:

Excerpt 71

If some people know more about it, uhm then those people should probably say more, and people who have nothing to contribute would le-, would get a lot more from it if they just sat back and listened to other people talk about it. But that's real hard to judge. I mean, I think at the very least everybody should have a little bit to say about it, uh people should solicit opinions of people who haven't spoken in order to see exactly where they are in the discussion. (junior faculty member)

Excerpt 71 begins to suggest that expertise should not be the sole criterion for deciding who should talk. In speculating about what makes discussions poor, a senior professor further explains why expertise as the sole criterion is problematic. "It becomes too much like a classroom when somebody takes over and becomes the teacher and uhm, uh you have a sense, you lose that sense of interchange, uhm then I think that makes bad intellectual discussion." Further:

Excerpt 72

I find it very hard to engage in a discussion on a topic about which I know nothing other than by, by asking questions. On the other hand, how much you know becomes a criterion then that becomes an inhibition too because nobody knows everything and uh, so a climate in which people uh, you know, can stick their necks out a little bit, which you can say things that are uninformed and somebody also will point out that they're uninformed uhm maybe, but that's okay. It's okay not to be informed uh and it's okay to be called on it. (senior faculty member)

The value of being willing to speak when one is uncertain about what he or she knows is further attested to by a graduate student.

Excerpt 73

I like it when people are pretty transparent and not afraid to make mistakes, willing to uhm take risks, willing to say I'm not sure uh, I understand that.

While being willing to risk making mistakes was seen as an attitude that contributed to good discussion, it was not without risks. In discussing his own self-presentational concerns, a graduate student had this to say:

Excerpt 74

I was very worried that I might say something and it would show that I didn't grasp everything . . . just worried about general issues, uh how I look and do I seem like a bright individual and have something to say, have original thoughts, any knowledge of well the field or just general classics? Or am I just a person who snuck in here and we're going to have to weed him out soon because there's really nothing upstairs.

Thus the beliefs about how expertise level should influence participation were partly contradictory. On the one hand it was believed that participation should be restricted to those who are informed and knowledgeable; on the other, that participation should be engaged in by everybody. Participants recognized that lively, involved interchange can only happen when people are not continuously self-censoring because they do not know enough. Yet it was simultaneously recognized that if participants routinely speak out of limited knowledge, the quality of the discussion might be "primitive." People both believed that good intellectual discussion requires a certain knowledge level and that discussion can become bad (uninvolving and lecturelike) when only experts can speak.

In a study of intellectual discussion in informal family conversations, Knoblauch (1991) identifies one of these dangers. He argues that discussions that get stuck "in the byways of instruction" become problematic. He describes the achievement of good discussion in this way:

The thrill of the dialectical complementarity of disagreement always faces dangerously in two directions: disagreement may lead to the establishment of asymmetries of knowledge (thus depriving "ignorants" of the right to disagree and thereby ruling out the equality of ping pong) and disagreement may lead into the troubled waters of conflict talk ending up with the opposite of sociability: shouting, crying, and quarrelling. (p. 187)

Talking about ideas among family members is a significantly different context from an academic one. Most noticeably, displays of knowledge and teaching sequences (Keppler & Luckmann, 1991) are not disvalued in the same way they may be in discussions among nonacademics. Among academics there is as much distaste for nonintellectual discussion (equal participation among ignorants) as there is for interaction that is not a discussion (one person delivering a lecture).

BELIEFS AS INDICATORS OF PARTICIPANTS' PROBLEM ANALYSIS

From interviews at University X, two sets of contrary beliefs were identified. Each belief about what is an appropriate way to act can be reframed as a situational problem analysis; that is, each belief about how one should communicate carries with it an implicit assessment of what participants see to be a routine way intellectual discussion in the academic context goes awry. I would argue, then, that academics are implicitly aware of four dangers (routine problems):

1a. Ideas are not challenged because the presenter possesses high institutional status.
1b. Ideas are criticized with insufficient recognition that the presenter is an inexperienced idea presenter/developer.
2a. Intellectual "discussion" becomes long-winded monologues displaying various participants' knowledgeability.
2b. "Intellectual" discussion becomes a fast paced, lively expression of ignorance and ill-informed opinions.

I would not argue that each of these problems is equally salient in all kinds of intellectual discussion. As was alluded to earlier, for instance, I think it likely that academics are more concerned to avoid Danger 2b—expressions of ignorance and ill-informed opinions—than are people in some other contexts. If so, we would expect that academic discussion groups will fall prey to Danger 2a (long-winded monologues) more often than will discussions in other contexts.

Let us return to the State U colloquium to consider how the expertise-equality dilemma was discursively displayed and managed.

7

Discursive Expressions of Institutional Rank

Glancing around the room at Tim's colloquium, State U participants notice an unfamiliar face: A not-so-young woman is sitting at the corner of the table. She appears to know Tim but no one else. Is she a student in another department? A faculty member? Ten minutes into the discussion period the woman raises her hand and is acknowledged by Tim. "This is a little outside of my expertise but I was wondering if there's a relationship between . . ."

She's a faculty member, colloquium participants conclude.

In interviews at State U, participants wanted to be seen as intellectually able but also wanted to avoid the impression that they were straining to display their own intellectual prowess. In addition, colloquium participants wanted to show, or at least to avoid calling into question, that they were acting appropriately for their institutional rank. In contrast to intellectual concerns, this concern was rarely mentioned explicitly; that is, participants did not say, "I want to be recognized as a full professor"; "I want to be seen as an advanced graduate student." An exception was one graduate student who in an interview said that in questioning fellow graduate students, "you don't want to raise yourself up to such a level that you're no longer a fellow graduate student." This comment is intriguing, for it implies that his concern was to *avoid* being seen as someone who was trying to claim a higher status than would be considered legitimate, rather than working to

insure that his existing status level was respected. Yet, although participants generally did not acknowledge that *they* wanted their institutional
rank recognized, they repeatedly discussed the need for participants to
talk to others in ways that took account of each participant's "experience."

In general, State U participants saw the colloquium as a situation in
which people came together with no person possessing special responsi-
bilities or prerogatives. The colloquium was not a classroom with a teacher;
participants were there because they cared about other members of the
community and wanted to talk about ideas. There was an ideal of equality,
even while both faculty and students recognized that it neither existed nor
was completely desirable. This ambiguity is well captured in Adam's (a faculty member) characterization of the role of graduate students. Graduate
students are:

Excerpt 75

peers or aspiring peers, they are learning to be faculty and/or other professionals and should be treated as such though there's the recognition at the
same time that they're not and uh, so there is that, the dual role. There is
that sorta apprenticeship, at the same time you know colleague as well. It's a
tough one, it doesn't always work out, that's for sure cause the power relationships are clear.

Faculty in the colloquium setting, in fact, did interactive work to minimize status differences and involve graduate students. As one faculty member noted, "I would almost never take the floor if I feel there are other
people, and particularly students, who have, uh, things they want to say."
This work to reign self in was a way faculty worked to combat status
inequality.

Yet outside of the colloquium participants were not equal. Graduate students were taught and evaluated by faculty, needed to get faculty members'
approval of actions they wanted to take, and generally were dependent on
maintaining the goodwill and approval of at least a subset of the faculty.
These institutional identities ostensibly were left at the door when people
came to colloquium. The colloquium was a place people came voluntarily
because they wanted to think and talk about issues important in communication. As I will show, however, institutional identities were not so easily
set aside. Instead they seeped into the discussion and commingled with the
more general intellectual identity concerns of all participants.

Conversational moves in this situation functioned simultaneously to
establish both institutional and intellectual identity. Earlier chapters
explored different aspects of intellectual identity, noting cooccurring rank
differences. This chapter focuses explicitly on institutional rank displays.

Described are how talk and silence patterns, questioning practices, and responses to noncomprehension enacted a participant as either a graduate student or a faculty member. Like Ochs (1993), I presume that enacting identity is best conceived as a bid by one individual to be taken as a certain kind of person. Thus the chapter's analyses show how in this setting these conversational practices functioned as recognizable and plausible bids that a person was either a graduate student or a faculty member. Following explication of these practices, their significance for the equality/expertise dilemma is explored. The chapter concludes by describing and analyzing the impact of a discussion rule instituted by the group to correct its perceived tilt toward expertise.

TALK AND SILENCE PATTERNS

Within this intellectual discussion group, the basic choice each communicator faced was to talk or to remain silent. However, members of the two main groups—graduate students and faculty—were not equally likely to make each choice. By and large, graduate students chose silence much more often than did faculty. When asked to characterize their role in colloquium, graduate students frequently referenced this silent state in a disparaging way. Ruth described her role as to be "a warm body," Trent said he was "a veg" and Jen expressed the hope that she would talk more ("Well hopefully I'll talk next semester"). In this situation, then, the act of being silent was both negatively valenced and associated with speakers possessing low institutional status. That silence typically goes with low status and interactional uncertainty has been documented by others (Rumelhart, 1983).

This association of silence with low institutional rank became problematic for discussants possessing higher institutional status. Brad, a tenured faculty member described himself as "a listener" and then went on to say:

Excerpt 76

Sometimes this semester here th-, say Brad Wilson you didn't say anything here on topics that were related to my background or interests, right and I said, Yeah, I kinda chose not to, it didn't mean I wasn't thinking of things but sometimes I choose not to say something.

Brad's spontaneous accounting for his silence—not something asked about by the interviewer—suggests he feels a need to overturn an inference that might be drawn about him. His disavowal ("It didn't mean I wasn't thinking of things") is interesting too, because it suggests what he takes to be a frequent meaning of a participant being silent. And while graduate students did not explain their silence in exactly this way, Brad's disavowal is consistent with the reasons they offered as to why they were often silent, a behavior they saw as motivated by their concern not to display inadequate understanding.

TYPES OF QUESTIONS

While graduate students did not talk as frequently as did faculty, they did talk. Like the faculty, they asked questions of presenters, but the kinds of questions they asked were not the same. Graduate students seemed less likely to make comments or ask questions that strongly challenged a presenter, and more likely to ask information questions. As with silence, faculty and graduate students regarded information questions as signaling a low intellectual level. Consider a remark Jason, a faculty member, made about fellow colloquium participants:

Excerpt 77

There are a lot of people that primarily ask questions, you know, try, looking for clarification when they do speak at colloquia so you know I, it doesn't give you a real good idea of how they think . . . there are a lot of people after almost a year and a half of being at colloquia, I just don't know how they think or what they think about or how smart they are . . . when they do talk it's basically: "I wasn't sure what you meant by that, could you tell me" or "Is that what you mean by?"

Jason's comment suggests a contrast between what many participants actually do and what they should do. Participants *should* talk in ways that reveal how they think and they *shouldn't* ask, at least exclusively, simple information questions. This negative loading on information questions is also revealed in Ann's (a graduate student) comment about her participation:

Excerpt 78

The questions I ask are in the main exploratory, explanation. I'm trying to sort out and make clear the information that I might not understand. I think that's probably unique among graduate students . . . they are very hesitant to ask questions that look like they don't know what is going on . . . I would rather understand than walk out with everyone thinking that "Gee, isn't she smart."

Ann does considerable work to make reasonable her asking of information questions. Her explanatory work cues that she regards these actions as

ones that the community might not value. If indeed, information questions are generally disvalued but are regarded as more acceptable from
participants lower in institutional status, then we might expect people with
higher institutional status to do more "work" when they ask an information
question.

Generally when graduate students asked information questions, they
did so straightforwardly or if apologies or disclaimers were present, they
acknowledged a possibility of not completely understanding something.
Below is a "typical" way graduate students formulated a question.

Excerpt 79

In the work that you did on checking to verify the Rogers and Farace scheme,
could you say it again, I think you said it near the end but I didn't quite catch
it. How did people's interpretations map against the claims they were making?

In contrast, people with higher levels of institutional status, particularly
when unknown to many of the participants of a group, would explicitly
preface and mark their asking of informational questions. At an all-day
seminar at a professional conference, one of the major participants asked
another:

Excerpt 80

I have, I have, uh a question about your, the paper . . . Uh, since I've not
done comparative analysis, it's sort of asked more for my own knowledge,
uhm and it's not a loaded question. Uhm some of the studies you refer to
specifically use the word sociability, others don't. What are the implications
of mixing these two kinds of studies?

If we assume that people do conversational work to head off negative
attributions, this question-asker evidences concern about two possible negative inferences. First, he seeks to legitimate why he, a person of at least
moderate rank, would ask a simple informational question. His remark
("I've not done comparative analysis, it's sort of asked more for my own
knowledge") makes salient that he has done other kinds of analyses and
that he has expertise of some sort. His comment also references, albeit in
a cryptic way, a logic of reasonable behavior; that is, a person must first
comprehend an idea before he or she can challenge it. Since this is a new
area, he is "reasonably" involved in working to understand it.

This is not the only negative inference the question-asker seeks to head
off. There is a second very different one cued by his comment, "and it's not
a loaded question." Since high-status question-askers are presumed to have

higher levels of intellectual ability, another possible interpretation of an informational question is that it is a wolf in sheep's clothing. Put another way, when a high status person asks a "simple question," it becomes plausible that the question may not be what it seems. It may be the first step in attempting to trap someone. Hence, the question-asker works to head off this negative attribution as well. This same move is described during a dissertation defense in a Greek university where a young male professor, outside of geology, prefaces a question to a female candidate in geology this way: "I would like to ask eh, simply so as to inform myself. . . ." (Pavlidou, 1991, p. 24). Pavlidou interprets this move as an attempt to reassure the candidate that the question is a real information one, not one meant to be nasty.

These prefacing moves not only head off negative attribution but themselves are markers of status. At a panel presentation at a communication conference, an audience member said to one of the presenters, "I'm not as familiar with this individual as you are. Let me ask a question that I don't have an answer for" (field notes). While I did not know this question-asker, the framing of the question led me to infer that he must be at least moderately high status. The preface suggested this because it displayed the question-asker as seeing it as noteworthy that he was asking an information question for which he did not have an answer. His formulation further implied that he does a lot of information questioning where he does possess the answer in advance, an activity common for teachers but not students. In this professional context, then, his use of this preface led me to infer that he was probably a professor of more than beginning rank. Prefacing moves were not common in the State U colloquium. They are most likely to occur when an individual's institutional rank is not known by the people in a group, such as was illustrated in the professional symposium or in the opening vignette of this chapter.[1]

In addition to using conversational prefaces when asking an informational question, faculty also used question types rarely displayed by graduate students. Among the most notable was the use of several subtle forms of "testing" questions. In classroom settings, teachers routinely ask students questions to which they already have answers. The format of these exchanges, initially described two decades ago (Sinclair & Coulthard, 1975), involves the teacher posing a question followed by a student response and then a teacher assessment of the response. Some educational scholars have been highly critical of the dominance of this kind of questioning type. For instance, Dillon (1988) writes; "Those who ask questions in school—teachers, texts, tests—are not seeking knowledge. Those who

---

[1]. The opening vignette is not based on a specific instance taken from the State U colloquium tapes. Rather, it reflects a recognizable instance of what I remember hearing at least several times over the years in which I participated.

would seek knowledge—students—are not asking questions at all. Classrooms are full of questions but empty of inquiry." (p. 115)

In a classroom where the focus is doing a lesson, questions asked by the teacher often have this testing purpose. Testing questions in intellectual discussion are considerably more subtle. The presenter is the conversational traffic manager, and the situation gives no one the structural rights to evaluate others' responses in the explicit way teachers do in a classroom. Nonetheless, two kinds of question formulations bring to mind this classroom testing function.

The first kind of question formulation makes visible its testing purpose through explicit discourse cues. In essence, the question asks the presenter to display particular pieces of knowledge.

Excerpt 81

[83-word preface] What made you decide to move in the way you did? And what are the pros and cons of going in your, in that direction?

Excerpt 82

But hasn't that been questioned? In other words what, what are the criticisms against precisely that statement that has been leveled—ask people for interpretations, you get 'em.

Excerpt 83

Eve: . . . That answer your question?

Ron: Well, I'd like to hear you talk more about what the criticisms are. And how you would take those into account in terms of interpreting the results?

Excerpts 81 through 83 come from an exchange between a faculty member, Ron, and a graduate student, Eve. In each excerpt, albeit in slightly different ways, Ron asks Eve to display that she has command of certain ideas and information. Of note is the way each question formulation turns our attention to whether Eve has the information rather than to the issue under discussion. By asking Eve for the "pros and cons," Ron's questioning calls to mind a test situation rather than one in which presenters have intellectual commitments and argue for one particular position. It is the kind of question teachers ask students to assess whether they understand the complexity of an issue. It is also a kind of question that a faculty member who is a student's advisor might ask to provide the student an opportunity to display his or her knowledgeability and command of certain ideas in front of significant others. Similarly, in Excerpts 82 and 83 we see Ron asking Eve to make the case against her position rather than making it himself and allowing her to respond to it (e.g., "But, if you ask people for interpretations, that's what you're going to get").

Another kind of questioning that cued itself as testing rather than information-seeking occurred when a questioner asked a presenter about an issue that all in the community knew to be a central part of the questioner's expertise area. In Excerpt 84, issue X was initially formulated as an issue of concern in a series of publications by the faculty questioner.

Excerpt 84

Sort of following up on that, uhm . . . I mean how do you know that this approach basically {issue X} is, is appropriate for a given theory?

The attribution that the question's primary purpose is testing flows from the implausibility that the questioner was actually seeking information about issue X.

When a question formulation makes visible that one person is testing another, the background institutional relationships become foregrounded. Because the right to test people is not equally distributed—teachers have that right; students do not—this kind of questioning implicates who the people must be.

A second format that reinforced and made visible existing institutional status was the use by a faculty member, almost always directed toward a student, of a string of relatively closed-ended questions. In the discussion period following a student presentation about motivation in the workplace, the following exchange occurred:

Excerpt 85

Student: . . . and there was a lot of interesting things that we have developed along the way as times have changed and purposes have changed. The truth of the matter

Faculty: I still don't know what's changed. What's changed?

Student: What's changed is the economic component that comprised the United States as a viable kind of capitalistic economy =

Faculty:	=so we're more entrepreneurial?
Student:	I think we are. I think you have to say that given that stat[
Faculty:	[and that means more bureaucracy?

This question format, a strategy that charitably might be labeled "Socratic questioning," or uncharitably, "grilling," implicitly invoked a classroom setting and the teacher-student role. Grilling questions (Socratic questioning) provide little maneuvering room but a lot of guidance, as a teacher might do in seeking to assist a student coming to the right answer. Similarly, a teacher interrupting a student's response before completion, as also illustrated in the above excerpt, might be appropriate in a classroom where the student is headed in a perceived wrong intellectual direction in a long-winded way.

The occurrence of testing and grilling questions and this type of interruption challenged the group's assumptive relational frame. Was the group truly a group of peers and near-peers talking with each other about ideas, the relational frame claimed in participants' self-reports? Or were the participants doing no more than enacting their institutional roles: a group of professors shaping, guiding, and evaluating graduate students, and a group of students working to please, or to avoid displeasing, those who exercised fate control over them?

RESPONSE TO NONCOMPREHENSION

A third kind of act that marked higher institutional status was the explicit admission of noncomprehension. Within the colloquium setting, it was common for participants, and especially novices (new graduate students), not to understand what was being said in the discussion. When novices did not understand a presentation, their typical response, as mentioned earlier, was to be silent. Jen, a student in her first semester of graduate school, gave this response when asked what concerns she had about her role in the colloquium:

Excerpt 86

Well, hopefully I'll talk next semester because there were times I wanted to say things but uh, I was too apprehensive.

One reason graduate students had concerns about speaking out is cued by Sally's explanation of why she often remained silent:

Excerpt 87

I'm afraid I might have missed something along the line that was obviously
attended to, and you know I was, just demonstrate how I spaced during one
part of the presentation by asking a question that's already been attended to.

Not all discussants kept silent about their failure to comprehend a presenter. Higher status participants (faculty members) did admit to not understanding what a presenter was saying. Immediately following a presentation
by Alison, an advanced Ph.D. student, Kevin, a faculty member, said:

Excerpt 88

Uh I I wish, I wish you could expl-, could explain, I have a question about two
things really that uh, uh, that I just didn't understand, uh you said uh, the
first is I wish you could read for me one more time, uh for us, the definition
of narrative that you're using. The second question uh relates to it, could you
explain a little bit more for me uhm what what you meant, the distinction
that you made in relations among stories and among narrative embeddings
I'm not sure I understand what you meant by that. And that the relation
between stories and surrounding narrative frames, it sounds very interesting
I just could not uh, I'm not sure what you mean.

In admitting to not understanding the speaker's point, Kevin has
implicitly treated his lack of understanding as news, something worth calling attention to. This is sensible to do only if one routinely understands
what is being discussed, a state typical only of experienced and higher status participants. Thus, an explicit admission of noncomprehension can be
seen to function as an implicit claim to having a high level of expertise. It
also can function as a criticism of the other's clarity.

That Kevin, in fact, attributes his lack of comprehension to the speaker
rather than to himself is evidenced by the way he repairs one of the
requests he makes. That is, he specifically asks Alison to define a key term
not just for him but for everybody ("could [you] read for me one more
time, uh for us"). In addition, his compliment ("it sounds very interesting") before his second statement of noncomprehension calls up the
image of a teacher who is trying to criticize constructively and is working
to say something positive before enumerating problems (Your definitions
and claims aren't clear). That in fact explicit admission of noncomprehension is a conversational device used by higher status participants to criticize the clarity of a lower status person becomes even more clear in the
exchange that follows between Kevin and Alison after she defines the several requested key terms:

Excerpt 89

Kevin: So that, so uh, well let me try one more time to get this
            straight in my head. It's me, it's not you I think.
Alison: No I think it's me.

Besides admitting again to not comprehending, Kevin attempts to
soften the implied criticism ("It's me, it's not you I think"). In saying this,
however, Kevin further suggests that everybody already sees the problem as
Alison's; that is, there would be no need for Kevin to say the problem was
his if he thought everyone was thinking so anyway; such a comment is sensible only if what is taken for granted needs to be overturned.

The possibility that explicit admission of noncomprehension can function simultaneously as criticism of another and as a claim to higher status
is further supported by an interview with a graduate student at University
X. In response to being asked about qualities thought essential to intellectual discussion, Raisa mentions feeling free to question and admit her
ignorance and proceeds to say:

Excerpt 90

I think the faculty is more willing to do that, some faculty more than others
are, I don't think graduate students are really feeling free to do that. And,
uhm, I see generally the more senior faculty being willing to do that, with the
implication that if *they* don't understand it hasn't been explained properly,
((laugh)) without ever the thought that they don't get it.

In addition to these three major manifestations, institutional identity
was made salient through a variety of less frequent communicative activities. Whenever participants engaged in discourse moves associated with or
only possible from one institutional role, they implied their institutional
identity. For example, when participants asked permission of another participant, asked for advice, sought help from a faculty member in answering
a question, explicitly referenced being a student in someone's class, referenced institutional activities such as preliminary exams or the dissertation
as being in the future, or excused the inability to answer a question by
explicit reference to "not having learned that yet," they implicated self as
having low institutional rank.

Similarly, higher institutional status was instantiated when participants
talked to another as if they were *the other's teacher*. Actions that invoked this
identity included: directing certain participants to pay attention to something and saying that it would be beneficial for a current or upcoming
class; giving advice, sometimes solicited but often unsolicited; making com-

ments about what students would face during the final stages of Ph.D. work or once they finished graduate school; encouraging certain participants to do something in the future or reprimanding them for not having done something yet; and talking about accomplishments of others who are identified as the participant's former students.

In this chapter I used the concept *institutional identity* to explain a host of conversational moves used by participants in intellectual discussion. Institutional identity work refers to conversational actions faculty and graduate students execute to support their institutional roles. A concern about institutional identity is concurrently other-oriented and self-oriented. That is, the conversational moves that establish the self as superior, equal, or subordinate are always done with regard to a conversational partner, and simultaneously establish how self regards the other.

IMPLICATIONS FOR THE EQUALITY-EXPERTISE DILEMMA

As noted earlier, participants at State U wanted to minimize the influence of institutional roles on their colloquium talk. In looking at the talk, one must conclude that they were only partly successful. A critical discourse scholar (e.g., Fairclough, 1992; van Dijk, 1993) might construe this as context-specific evidence that those with power do what they can to maintain their power over those with less of it. I do not entirely dispute this interpretation; I do, however, think it inadequately captures important aspects of the situation.

That participants were of different institutional ranks, differing in substantive and argumentative expertise, was a fact of the situation. This fact intersected with State U's ideal of the colloquium as an equal situation. The tangled nature of the group's commitments to equality and expertise is poignantly marked in a joke made by Steve, a faculty member, when he was asked by a graduate student interviewer what the role of graduate students should be in colloquium.

Excerpt 91

Sit there and shut up! No, no, just a joke, just a joke. What is their role? (pause) I think their role should be just as much as close as possible to the faculty role as anything, that they should leap in with whatever's on their mind, in terms of questions and things they want to say in reaction, on how it relates to their own ideas, or their own work, as far as seeing problems with the research.

Steve's comment goes to the heart of the expertise-equality dilemma. His thoughtful and elaborated response after rewording the interviewer question ("What is their role?") suggests he was sincere in labeling his opening comment as a joke. The substance of his answer displays his commitment to equality. On the other hand, it is difficult to discount his initial response ("sit there and shut up") as only a joke and hear it as other than a not-so-subtle reminder of who's who in the situation. Thus, the group's recognition of expertise differences and what that implied, and its corresponding commitment to achieving equality, jockeyed with each other in uneasy tension.

Any communicative action that implicated communicators' institutional rank could be judged fitting and appropriate, or it could be seen as another inappropriate display of inequality. By and large, State U regarded its participation patterns as a problem. The group regarded the fact that faculty talked a lot and graduate students only a little as an undesirable feature of its colloquium. Participants wanted a more equal environment. In service of that goal, the group instituted a discussion rule, which at the time of the interviews had been in place about a year.

THE FIVE MINUTE RULE

In place at the time of the interviews was an interactional practice the State U group called "the five minute rule." The five minute rule specified that in the first five minutes following the conclusion of a presentation, only graduate students could ask questions or make comments. As in a race in which a younger or less skilled runner is given a head start, the five minute rule sought to give graduate students a head start. Graduate students were given a short time to talk without competition from faculty, a practice expected to facilitate their continued talking after faculty entered the discussion.

After a year's experience with the rule, State U participants were disenchanted. Although interviewees felt that the rule had come into existence for good reasons, all participants felt the rule was not "working well." Consider faculty member, Jim's response:

Excerpt 92

I think it's a good idea but it doesn't work. In other words it seems a little too contrived to me, and I think students feel it's contrived. And as a result there's a pressure about it rather than a spontaneous flow. It's kind of like the rule was built on the assumption that these graduate students have things to say and questions to ask, but they don't ((laughs)) . . . The rule's put up and no one says anything so there's this awkward silence when someone says "Well, is it over yet? Can someone jump in?" And it just leaves a real sort of awkward feeling . . . I'd find it a little demeaning in some ways if I were a graduate student. I wouldn't want it. I would want to know that I could speak and that people would give me the chance to be called on. And you know if I wanted to interrupt, I could interrupt. But I wouldn't want the rule cause it feels like "go ahead graduate students, ask your stuff first and get it out of the way."

Graduate students also disliked the rule.

Excerpt 93

I don't know, it seems to segregate graduate students in a way that seems to me, I don't know, it might have a thwarting effect. You know cause it kinda puts us on the spot (   ) It segregates us. It separates the audience . . . On the other hand you can see the reason why [the rule was instituted] cause you can have faculty talking and arguing with each other, and not letting graduate students.

Excerpt 94

Awkward as hell. Um, no I know why it was instituted. I, I think that it makes sense, the reasons behind instituting it were valid. But it is awkward. I would rather see who's ever the colloquium chief, the colloquium chief should take more of an, an active part in directing the discussion as far as graduate students are concerned. In other words realizing that it can be difficult for graduate students to get a word in edgewise if the faculty gets all heated up about something, or whatever. Instead of having this five minute rule, just be aware of that and give graduate students an opportunity when they indicate that they want it, not blanket, not you know always, but yeah, give them the chance. Not necessarily in the first five minutes of colloquium but throughout.

Uniformly, faculty and graduate students felt the rule was not accomplishing what it was intended to do. As one faculty member noted, "At this point, it's a bit of an embarrassment. There's got to be a better way."

In seeking to make the discussion situation more equal, the State U group had introduced a structural solution—regulating talk rights at certain times. This solution, however, rather than solving the problem, created new ones. Perhaps this rule would have been more effective if the five minutes reserved for graduate students occurred at the end of the session. At least in this case, the graduate students would have had an opportunity to talk *after* the conversation got moving. In allocating the first five minutes to students, the group failed to recognize the inherent difficulties in beginning discussion. That is, not only do discussants need to sort through what a presenter has said before they can formulate what they want to ask, but the first question is by its very placement highly visibile. Thus, even before the five minute rule, the first few minutes in State U's colloquium had frequently been halting and a bit awkward. With the five minute rule in place, graduate students became visibly responsible for discussion at the discussion's most difficult moment.

The problem with the five minute rule was more fundamental than where it was placed, however. In seeking to combat inequality through a structural practice that extended rights (or a responsibility) to persons based on their institutional identity, the five minute rule reified what the group was seeking to overcome: the distinction between faculty members and graduate students.

The equality-expertise dilemma was not the only problem with which the group struggled. State U also struggled about suitable ways to express emotion. Let us examine what they believed.

8

Emotion in Intellectual Talk

In academic disciplines, as in political parties, a good blazing row is as capable of arousing vicarious enjoyment as it is of damaging credibility and reputation . . . When people's ideological identities are at stake, passions run deep. (Becher, 1989, p. 98)

Is passion good or to be avoided? What exactly do academic groups believe about emotion? Drawing upon the interviews at State U and University X, this chapter looks at beliefs about three sets of issues: (a) the understood relationships among emotion, ideas, and people, (b) topic abstraction and emotional involvement, and (c) the ideal emotional climate for colloquia. For each, we again see a dilemmatic logic at work.

EMOTIONS, IDEAS, AND PEOPLE

At an abstract level, the role of emotion in intellectual talk does not appear to be dilemmatic. Academics agreed that passion about ideas and involvement with issues was to be desired, and they agreed that feelings of defensiveness, hostility, and personal attack of others were to be avoided.

Excerpt 95

I think that, uh, it helps if people care somewhat passionately about the ideas that's uh, being discussed. When you [the author] came in and talked about intellectual discussion in colloquium, now I happen to care about that, but it was clear to me that you cared about it and so our responses seemed to be working toward the engagement of something that was significant to us. Um hmm and you seemed open to the legitimacy of challenge if, if you were going to defend your point of view or whatever, it wasn't a sense that the defenses were going up before the uh, conversation hit your ears. (University X, senior faculty member)

Excerpt 96

I think that part of that is, we as humans are emotional beings so the good part would be to be animated, to be somewhat heated if necessary. Or to say well no, I don't really get that I'm following where you're going . . . Bad would be where it becomes an attack on another person, or what another person said . . . being as I said, "Well that was just stupid" or bringing in that attack kind of emotion. (University X, junior faculty member)

In addition, absence of feelings and involvement were recognized as undesirable. In response to a question about the qualities of poor intellectual discussion, a senior faculty member said:

Excerpt 97

Well let's see, what is bad intellectual discussion? Uh one that is boring. That's probably the worst. The worst thing you could say about intellectual discussion was that it was boring. (University X)

Simply put, participants believed that expression of certain feelings (i.e., passion about ideas) was appropriate and suppression of other kinds (e.g. attack of a person) was needed. At first glance, this may appear a reasonable way of distinguishing appropriate from inappropriate emotion. If, in fact, it is possible to separate people from the ideas about which they talk, then we have a straightforward undilemmatic ideal, but if ideas and people cannot be cleanly separated, then these rules about emotional action become suspect.

In intellectual discussion people and ideas are unavoidably and intimately intertwined.[1] That academics, themselves, recognize this intertwined relationship is evidenced at several places in the interviews. For instance, consider two responses from State U faculty members to the

---

[1] Albrecht and Hall (1991) argue for a similar relationship between ideas and people in a medical center where a department is considering different kinds of innovation.

following question: "Every week there are different topics followed by a discussion. To what degree do you think the issues that come up in the colloquia are the same across weeks? If so, what are they?"

Excerpt 98

Well uh, funny. I picture people rather than issues. I picture Dan and Jim Smith and Lisa. And you know it's funny I've forgotten what the issues are. I just remember the people.

Excerpt 99

Well, let's see. They kinda, kind of come down to people don't they? ((said laughing)) I mean uh Lisa, you know will see tensions between multiple concerns and will ask something coming from that angle. Uh Kim will, uh ask you, uh how its really developing moment by moment. You're glossing the thing, you're looking at it in this big uh, in this generalized way but how does it really happen? How is it experienced by the people who are doing it, moment to moment construction. John will raise the metaquestion, ah self-reference.

Rather than answering the question using the frame supplied by the researcher (recurring issues), each interviewee challenges the assumption presupposed by the question. The possibility that the participants recognize that their "people" answers may be challenging what is presupposed by the question is suggested by the initial preface "well," a token frequently used to preface disagreement (Schiffrin, 1987). More importantly, whereas one interviewee proceeds to explicitly talk about the two as a single unit (Excerpt 99), the other suggests that the only way to identify issues is through people, the memorable units! (Excerpt 98).

At University X the recognition that ideas and people are deeply connected is visible in several graduate students' remarks. In response to a question about how good and bad discussion could be distinguished, graduate student Jeff said:

Excerpt 100

Well the way people treat each other, uhm often arguments do nothing for intellectual discourse. It's personal instead of saying, there's a problem with an idea, you say, "you're stupid." The intellectual discourse is not going to continue. The person's going to shut down. They'll stop definitely. It means that people are not going to trust. People are not going to get trust out of you. You'll often hear, and I've probably said this somewhat myself, I just said it, that ideas can be separate from the person. But it's hard. If it's your idea, you're going to feel it's a part of you. Part of you is in there. It's impossible to completely separate the idea. The ideal is impossible.

In focusing on the role of criticism and praise, graduate student Tim offered this comment:

Excerpt 101

I think praise is a means of bringing people into discussion, just like criticism can be a way of driving them out. That doesn't mean that praise should be given indiscriminately, but again if there is a way. *I just got myself in a hole here,* saying if there's a way to praise the ideas of the person who has the idea so that they can take ownership of the praise. But at the same time I say if someone's criticized, aren't they still going to take that very personally? I don't know. Criticize me now!

Both Tim and Jeff struggle to articulate what they think. They contradict themselves, try to reconcile the contradictions, and work to place an official solution (to criticize the idea, not the person) in the context of their actual experiences. The paradoxes become apparent. Intellectual discussion requires disagreement and criticism; discussion is not intellectual without these features. Yet at the same time, criticism of an idea carries a potential to destroy the discussion by wounding the person who offered the idea.

In commenting on a lack of liveliness in the University X departmental colloquia, a graduate student explicitly suggested that a problem arose because group members did not want to hurt others' feelings.

Excerpt 102

There's a hesitancy to push people on their ideas, which for me, I'm scared of that, so it's not all a bad thing, but uhm, and somehow it seems like doing that comes out feeling hostile or something, you know, like someone is being disagreeable, you know, or inconsiderate, I don't know what, putting people on the spot . . . Occasionally we get into a good discussion but a lot of times it's like, well I think this, and this person thinks this, I think that. And we're all kind of agreeing and skipping around but there's not really any engagement in issues or ideas.

The difficulty in finding appropriate ways to express emotion is further complicated by what participants take to be operating institutional beliefs about the role of emotion in intellectual talk.

Excerpt 103

What I think of as uhm a *typical intellectual discussion* I'd say that the drive is toward not expressing your feelings and that is seen as a better, a better way to handle intellectual discussion but I find it enriches it a lot when people do talk about things that they're invested in. (graduate student)

Excerpt 104

Well *the ideal view*, once again, is that it shouldn't involve feelings really because it's about your ideas and you don't want to attack people. In the real ideal I suppose you wouldn't have positive feelings attached to the ideas and when an idea's found to be good, you shouldn't take joy in any of it because it's just an idea. But in reality I think they're essential for building that climate for a good intellectual discussion. People ought to feel good about their intellectual discussion, about themselves, or good about going into the situation. So they're essential, essential to the intellectual venue. It's like a building, a prerequisite for a good intellectual discussion, a pretty positive feeling. (graduate student)

While no participant believed emotional expression was inappropriate in intellectual talk, participants nonetheless spoke as if this was what was believed by most academics. This is evidenced through the way the graduate students contrasted their own view with what they called the "typical view" or "the ideal view." Participants saw the academy's view as one in which emotion and reason were at odds; feeling and thinking did not go together. Elvin, a senior faculty member, discusses the falseness of this dichotomy directly:

Excerpt 105

I'm not sure where you draw the line between ideas and feelings exactly. Uh I think uh part of what makes intellectual discussion fun and valuable is I mean, the sense of engagement is, arises from people really caring about what they're saying. And so there is a kind of passion that goes with, with uh, saying what you think/feel. Right I mean what's the difference? At some point, uh in other words you think that what you're saying is right, right? And that's not just thinking, that's a feeling uh you know, and so even at that level I don't think I could distinguish between saying what you think and expressing your feelings.

At the level of framing the activity, participants believed their own personal views toward emotion were at odds with what was generally believed. This is stated explicitly in comments 103 and 104 and is implied by Elvin's comment. Elvin goes to considerable lengths to argue for the impossibility and undesirability of separating feelings and ideas. Such elaboration makes sense only if an opposite belief is presumed to be the reigning common wisdom.

As was noted earlier, participants did not hold disparate beliefs about the role of emotion. All believed passion and involvement were good, and defensiveness and attack were bad. Nevertheless, once one grants the difficulty, if not impossibility, of separating ideas and people during intellectual discussion, then a contradiction becomes apparent. It is not clear how one can display emotion about ideas but not about people. When speakers are passionate about ideas, there is always risk that their actions will be seen as self-defensive or hostile. At the same time, when speakers edit out strong feelings—particularly negative ones toward another's idea, or positive ones toward one's own—this makes a discussion boring. Thus, the group beliefs about how to manage emotional expression during discussion cannot escape being contrary.

Not all types of intellectual discussion foreground the link between persons and ideas. For instance, when an academic group talks about a socially controversial issue or a book written by an absent author, everyone present is likely to be not only at some distance, but relatively equidistant, from the focal idea. In such cases, the awareness of person-idea links decreases, and exploring and reacting to the focal idea becomes more central. In this kind of discussion, however, a different kind of interactional tension surfaces.

TOPIC ABSTRACTION AND EMOTIONAL INVOLVEMENT

As a number of scholars have documented (e.g., Gamson, 1992; Tannen, 1989), involvement with an issue of discussion is conversationally marked by relating ideas to a person's own experiences. Telling a story, recounting an example, or giving a personal anecdote are the ways people display interest and investment in an issue. Lower levels of involvement are cued by talking about an idea in an abstract and detached fashion. If passion about ideas is valued, the dominant way academics talk about ideas in colloquia should make liberal use of personal examples and stories, but they do not. Why, we might ask, do people who value passion about ideas so often talk in an abstract and decontextualized style? The answer, I believe, lies in the potential identity risks associated with an involved style. Simply put, a personal anecdote and an abstract statement are not perceived as being equally intellectual. The risks of being judged nonintellectual are far greater to one who expresses experiential knowledge than in expressing abstract knowledge. If one seeks to be seen as intellectual, a tangential story is a more serious interactional error than a tangential abstract statement ever will be. Consider a faculty member's response to a question about what kinds of colloquium behavior she found particularly unimpressive:

Excerpt 106

When it seems the only thing they know is their own experience, the only thing they have to add is a personal anecdote, and they don't know what, they either don't know or they can't say what the connection is between that and some broader idea. (junior faculty member, University X)

The fact that not all knowledge is equally valued is given attention in junior faculty Cecile's reflection about how the colloquium group may view her:

Excerpt 107

I really think about how people might perceive me after having heard the seven comments I've made during the year. If from that people have drawn inferences that I perceive the world experientially, you know, because I quote things from {name}, or I quote things from, that could be because I, *they better not write me off because of that.* That makes me mad and that's a fear of mine. (junior faculty member, University X)

Cecile's fear that she will be written off makes sense if indeed not all kinds of knowledge are valued equally.[2] Although participants did not comment about this much, their widely shared definition of intellectual discussion as talk about ideas of moderate abstraction points to a tension

---

2. The interviews did not have sufficient numbers of men and women at each institutional rank to address the issue of whether a concern to tie the life world to the abstract is more typical of female academics than of males. Belenky, Clinchy, Goldberger, and Tarule (1986) in their investigation of women's ways of knowing make the distinction between connected knowing (learning and arguing from personal connections) and constructed knowing (integrating the connected with the abstract, "out there" kinds of knowledge). My impression from years in the academy is that although many academics are committed to constructed knowing, somewhat more women than men are so committed. Compared to male academics, females are likely to experience a greater conflict between the culture's definition of what it means to be an intellectual and the culture's gender expectations. This tension, I would suggest, leads women academics to reflect explicitly about what it means to know, and in turn women develop more elaborated conceptions of the desirable relationship between the life world and the abstract than do men.

that must confront discussants. The tension is this: Should academics talk in ways that promote their own and others' involvement with ideas (tie the abstract to the particular), or should they talk in ways that minimize the danger of being judged nonintellectual (be abstract)? The fact that this is a dilemma academics do face is captured well in the following faculty comment:

Excerpt 108

Well on this example thing, I think it's often seen as nonintellectual because anybody can do it. The washerwoman can tell a story about her life that might even be relevant to a topic, but it's a greater intellectual skill to deal with it abstractly without referring to everyday life. I don't happen to agree with that but I think it's often perceived that way. The more abstract you are, the smarter you are. And uh, whereas I think the real insight is to see the connections between your everyday life and these abstract ideas. (junior faculty member, University X)

A final problem colloquium groups face concerns the kind of emotional climate to be promoted.

THE GROUP CLIMATE: SERIOUS OR PLAYFUL?

Intellectual discussion, by definition, is serious talk about ideas that have more than local, person-specific importance. It is also, as I have shown, an evaluative context; each person knows that every other person will be drawing conclusions about self's intellectual and emotional mettle. At State U, the seriousness of the occasion was reinforced further by marking the colloquium a public occasion. Announcements appeared in a weekly campus paper inviting any and all to attend. Also, although attendance from outsiders was not typical, the possibility of nondepartmental attendees was part of the situation definition. While intellectual discussion is expected to be serious, however, it is also expected to be enjoyable. David, a faculty member at University X, articulated this expectation especially strongly:

Excerpt 109

It does bother me . . . when people get very very serious about, I don't know, some trend in research there or theory that they don't like, or about the importance of being dedicated or something so that it gets heavy-handed. I'm very much for having fun. And if I'm not having fun, I'm not having fun. You know, why am I doing it? It's not fun.

It was not merely that fun was desired—an intensity of sentiment not everyone expressed—but that participants sought to escape the dangers of discussion that got "too serious." Humor was seen as an effective way to do this. In talking about ways to foster good discussion, at a slightly earlier point in this same interview, David explicitly identifies the values of humor.

Excerpt 110

It's sort of like a release of tension about the fact that there's a conflict between people and they're battling over some ideas for the time being. Or ah, how people are feeling about their role in the group or something else. It kind of like acknowledges that when people giggle because they somehow recognize some incongruity there, that influences it. And I think that's, humor is one good way of letting it out, kind of taking some of the impact out of things that can get too serious. (faculty member, University X)

The typical danger in this kind of discussion situation is that the talk may be perceived as becoming too serious. When this happens, individuals become preoccupied with what is at stake for self. In such situations, people tune out of the ongoing discussion to plan out what they will say. In preplanning rather than formulating on the spot, participants lessen the risk of saying something that can be thought really stupid. At the same time, they become part of creating a discussion in which people are making mini-speeches on an issue rather than responding in a moment-to-moment way to what others are saying. Thus, a playful environment is not only less threatening but is essential for serious discussion to happen.

I have highlighted the danger of discussion that becomes too serious, and while it is generally the more prominent danger, it is not the only one. Discussion can get too playful. After acknowledging the importance of maintaining a good balance between playfulness and seriousness, Matt made the following comment:

Excerpt 111

While it's good to be playful uhm, about the research you're doing, the work you're doing, and not take yourself or it overly seriously, that uh, that, that you can go too far with it. You need to take yourself and your research seriously enough that it merits being taken seriously by other people. And also that some of what we're talking about is serious stuff. (State U, faculty member)

In sum, excessive playfulness can undermine the community's understood central purpose—to engage in serious intellectual talk. At the same time, if the discussion frame gets too serious, participants lack the emotional safety that promotes interactional comfort and enables spontaneous responsiveness to others.

PARTICIPANTS' PROBLEM ANALYSES

Participants considered emotion essential for good intellectual talk, yet they also regarded emotion as destructive and inappropriate. Just as participants' contrary beliefs about equality and expertise could be reformulated as problems of which academics are aware, the same can be done for beliefs about emotion. With regard to emotion in intellectual talk, academics seem aware of three sets of dangers.

3a. Feelings toward an idea are expressed and they are perceived/meant to be attacking of other or defensive of self.

3b. Feelings toward an idea are suppressed (or not experienced), and the discussion is boring and lifeless.

4a. Discussion is so abstract that conversational engagement is inhibited.

4b. Discussion is so concrete that a definition of the situation (or person) as intellectual is challenged.

5a. The emotional climate of the group is so playful that sustained engagement with issues is undermined.

5b. The emotional climate is so serious that participants do not engage with issues of the discussion moment but rather they utter intellectual set pieces.

How did State U manage these tensions? What conversational strategies were used to minimize the dangers of emotion in intellectual talk?

9

Intellectual Community

How would you explain colloquium to someone outside the department?

Excerpt 112

Oh I would say, "Do you want to come to our colloquium?" We, um, have a pretty unique little thing going there. Uh graduate students and faculty all kinda get together, trade ideas ( ), sometimes have outside speakers who are interesting but most often it's us and uh, we can really get a pretty good idea who we are and what we're like. And uh, every once in a while we get some really terrific topic going. And sometimes we get people who are really informative, and so on. In other words, I would probably do a sell job.

((Interviewer: And the key thing you would sell?))

Well there aren't too many intellectual communities at State U. That's what I would sell. A unique intellectual community. (faculty member)

In this exchange, faculty member John invokes "intellectual community" to mark an accomplishment of the colloquium group. John frames the colloquium as achieving (or coming close to) a sought-after but difficult-to-achieve interactional state. The colloquium is more than a weekly meeting. It is a demarcated group of people coming together regularly to get to know each other's intellectual concerns ("most often it's us, uh and we can really get a pretty good idea who we are and what we're like"). In describing the colloquium group this way, John is praising the group.

As a term, *community* has several meanings, only one of which is as a term of praise. When paired with adjectives like *speech* (Hymes, 1974) or *discourse* (Bizzell, 1992; Swales, 1990), the term *community* is a relatively descriptive one pointing to an identifiable set of people. Thus, a working-class neighborhood or a Native American reservation may be described as a speech community[1]; a group of stamp collectors or an academic discipline may be described as a discourse community. While it was clear that the colloquium group, as a manifestation of an academic discipline, is a discourse community, John appears to be claiming more for the colloquium group than this.

Somewhat closer to John's implied meaning is the definition mediator Carl Moore gives for community.

> Community exists when people who are interdependent struggle with the traditions that bind them and the interests that separate them in order to realize a future that is an improvement upon the present. (Moore, 1994, p. 199)

John's usage of the term *community* calls up more than people who struggle together; it implies a certain amount of success in the struggle. Community, as John invokes it, implies a group of people who care about, and support, each other as they jointly pursue intellectual aims. His usage evokes a group in which motives are relatively pure and a sense of community is the result. That is, this group has successfully accomplished a state of being enabling it to combat the extreme individualism and self-preoccupation that Bellah and his colleagues (Bellah, Madsen, Swidler, & Tipton, 1985, 1992) describe as so prevalent in U.S. society.

Assessment of how well any group meets an ideal is likely to yield differences of opinions because group members are likely to have had different experiences. At State U participants disagreed about whether their colloquium deserved to be credited as a well-functioning community. Faculty member Joan described the colloquium as "a weak version of a social occasion. You can count on seeing a bunch of people regularly. I wouldn't go so far as to say a community." In saying "I wouldn't go so far as to say a community," Joan distinguishes the actual state of affairs in the colloquium from the desired one. Furthermore, her formulation tells us that she sees the actual occasion to be a distance from the ideal. While her comment focuses on the way the group fails to meet the ideal, it nonetheless implies the salience and applicability of the ideal. If no

---

[1.] For example, see Philipsen (1990) for description of a working-class Chicago community; Heath (1983) for descriptions of black and white Southern working-class communities. Basso (1979) and Philips (1983) provide examples of Native American speech communities.

one in the colloquium group pursued intellectual community, or thought that the group was achieving it, a comment about the group "not achieving" it would seem bizarre and irrelevant.

Other State U participants saw the colloquium as coming closer to the ideal than Joan did.

Excerpt 113

I think uh there's, I don't know whether you'd call it a social function to it but there is certainly like a community function. That's like a time when all of us meet each week. Uh papers, even when we know that we're not interested . . . in what's being presented we'll all try to show up as support, as just something we do together as a department each week. (graduate student)

Excerpt 114

It's kind of a symbol of um, of unity. It's to give us some cohesiveness, and that the graduate students and the faculty can come together and meet, um, sorta on equal ground. Um you know which I think is valuable and something that I, I wish had gone on at the two places I did my graduate work. (faculty member)

State U's colloquium did not fully meet criteria for an ideal community: The discussion group had instances of nastiness, personal self-aggrandizing, and uneven commitment from its members. Moreover, how far the group was from the ideal—just a little bit or a moderate distance—was a matter of dispute. It seemed that faculty and graduate students who had positive relationships with key departmental members (i.e., the department chair, the most visible senior professor) were more likely to feel positive than those who did not. Nonetheless, even recognizing the legitimacy of these opinion differences, the colloquium group was sufficiently successful at enacting community to merit a careful examination of its practices.

A number of communicative features both contributed to and marked the presence of community at State U. One important feature, described in chapter 2, was the group's reflection about, and management of, the interactional dilemma: Should participants ask easy or tough questions? As noted before, there was no straightforward answer to this question. Easy questions could be seen as supportive and caring, or they could be taken as evidence that one did not respect another sufficiently to engage with the other in a serious manner. Difficult questions could be a sign of intellectual respect, or could be perceived as being used to hurt another and show off. In the rest of the chapter, I describe three other practices that contributed to intellectual community in State U.'s departmental colloquium. In the next chapter, I argue why these practices are key to managing the problems of emotional expressiveness.

CONVERSATIONAL PRACTICES
THAT MARKED FRIENDLINESS AND TRUST

Through the ways people talk with each other, they evince whether they are friendly or distant. At the State U colloquium, four conversational practices contributed to the sense that this was a group of people among whom there was goodwill and some amount of trust. A first practice participants used was to do idea-crediting in asking a question or making a remark.

Excerpt 115

Um this is kind of following, maybe you could *see it as following up on Frank's question* about perceptions . . . (faculty member)

Excerpt 116

Um, yeah I, *on a similar theme as Ralph's,* I have down the characters and, but when I watched it, here was a person who especially in the humor was coming off as something else. And I wasn't able in that short time to characterize . . . (faculty member)

In crediting how a question links to the prior talk, speakers are making visible how what they say is tied to what has gone before; that is, idea-crediting facilitates conversational coherence. Yet if linkage clarity were the only purpose, it could be done without referencing the person who made the specific remark. In mentioning a specific speaker in a question preface, the questioner validates the previous speaker's contribution as reasonable or interesting. Such actions deliver a low-level affirmation to the person mentioned, and establish that the group values comments and questions being interactionally responsive.

Related to idea-crediting was a second practice: noting how one's comments in the here and now related to outside colloquium conversations with community members.

Excerpt 117

One final point and then I'm gonna shut up. *Reid Hillerman and I had a big argument about a month ago* in which he said, "What oh we've gotta do is tell the American people what a liberal is . . ." (faculty member)

Excerpt 118

No, I think that uh, uh I think that it does, but the problem still for me is locating outside that interaction. *I told this to Linda the other week* . . . But I think it's artificial for the researcher to say an aggregate cultural dimension's, reality, we just pose that as reality. *And as I was talking to Martin before, this morning* and I said I think that's making the phenomena fit the tool . . . (graduate student)

By referring to conversations outside the colloquium, participants made visible that they had ongoing relationships with each other where they continued to talk about ideas. Talk about ideas was not merely a colloquium activity; it was something that people did with each other in an ongoing way. These kinds of referencing practices make visible, and further affirm, the existence of connections among group members.

A third practice, which in some other contexts has been described negatively, was speaking for another.[2] Participants spoke for others and said what they thought others were trying to say (i.e., what they were thinking).

Excerpt 117

I think Sherry's point is that uh, people, one aspect, people might be cultural categories whether they like it or not.

Excerpt 118

I don't understand what you're saying. *I think what Chris is saying,* I see different companies really setting in place assumptions about individuals in the company that then managers . . .

[2.] Mind reading in introductory interpersonal communication text books (e.g., Knapp, 1978) has often been described as a destructive practice in close relationships. In contrast, Schiffrin (1993) labels the practice "speaking for another," Based on analysis of conversational exchanges, she shows how this practice has a number of positive interactional functions.

Speaking for another is a conversational strategy that is presumptive unless people know each other well. The attempt to articulate what another is saying in a group in which all have the same message input, is equivalent to claiming a background familiarity with the other. Thus speaking for another, similar to outside conversational references, pointed to the existence of connections among people that extended beyond the immediate interactional context.

A final way discourse practices made the existence of community visible was through the common occurrence of think-aloud speech. This practice was sometimes explicitly legitimated with mini-accounts, as was seen in Excerpts 33 and 34, but often was just done. Think-aloud speech is talk whose nonfluency and repair level suggest that a person is working through what he or she thinks right there on the spot. Many instances of the discussion discourse at State U exemplified throughout the book illustrate this quality. Analysis of an interdepartmental faculty symposium at State U provided a noticeable contrast. In this high- visibility symposium, with many participants who had not known each other previously, repairs and reformulations were far less common. Discussion remarks were lengthy, suggesting that the participant had preplanned what he or she was going to say and was looking for a topically suitable place to launch a mini-speech (see Appendix C).

Greene and his colleagues (Greene, Lindsay, & Hawn, 1990) have demonstrated that speakers who have time to preplan a message, even if only briefly, will be considerably more fluent than those who do not. Thus, when speakers are as halting and nonfluent as many of the comments from State U illustrate, the impression left is that not a lot of prepackaged contributing went on. This, in turn, implicitly marked the discussion situation as one in which people were comfortable and trusting enough to be willing to allow others to witness them thinking in the rough and unpolished way that first thoughts often emerge.

THE PRACTICE OF HUMOR

Humorous comments and group laughter were frequent occurrences in State U's colloquium. Common sites for these actions were at the start of a presentation and upon the opening of the questioning/discussion period. Being the presenter at colloquium, as one participant put it, was being in the "hot seat," a position that brought potential risks of embarrassment. A presenter's fears of embarrassment and experience of discomfort were frequently shared with the group via a mocking comment made by the presenter to which the group typically responded with laughter.

For instance, at the conclusion of her presentation, a graduate student said:

Excerpt 121

Questions? ((pause)) So perfectly delivered that no one has any questions.
((*group laughter*))
[questioning begins]

Another example of this kind of humorous marking is displayed in Andrea's opening remarks. Andrea had completed a master's degree at State U several year earlier. She had then gone to another institution for her doctoral work but had kept contact with several faculty members. During a departmental visit, she had agreed to give a colloquium on her dissertation research and began it saying:

Excerpt 122

Andrea: And Jef [the colloquium coordinator] has told me that there haven't been any fireworks. You've been a very tame, uh, colloquium, uh audience prior to this time. I'm just encouraging you to keep it up.
((*group laughter*))
Jef: I've been using a whip and chair.

While this kind of comment was more common among graduate students, faculty also made them. At the start of his presentation, Scott said the following:

Excerpt 123

In conclusion I think
((*group laughter*))
Okay, uh okay I think I'm ready now . . . [presentation begins]

Of note is the way these comments point to discomforts in the presenting role. In responding with collective laughter, the group both acknowledges and legitimates presenters' feelings of discomfort. In essence, the laughter marks the group's sharing of a view of the presenter role, that it's hard work and understandably threatening. However, because the group proceeded to engage in the kind of questioning/discussion that generated these comments, it simultaneously affirmed the group's valuing of, and commitment to, serious engagement.

While humorous remarks about the presenter role were most frequently made by graduate students, humorous remarks about others' idiosyncrasies or minor incompetencies were most frequently made by faculty members and directed at each other. At one point in a discussion, faculty member Jane had made a confusing and incoherent comment. She concluded her comment by asking the presenter in a laughing voice, "Can you figure out the question?" to which the group responded with loud laughter. A short time later in this same discussion, faculty member Jim offered the following interjection into Alan's question:

Excerpt 124

Alan: Yeah uh I'm still working on formulat-, formulating this question clearly
Jim: Try a Jane Jefka
((*loud group laughter*))
Alan: I'm trying to figure out . . .

While much of the humor that occurred was of this one-liner interjection type, on some occasions playfulness occurred over a more extended exchange. Excerpt 125 illustrates such an occasion. This exchange occurred at a highly face-threatening juncture. Jesse, a student presenter, had been challenged by Fred (faculty member) for buying into the values of business and management unthinkingly. Fred also accused Jesse of encouraging employees to put on an interactional facade and just insure that employees "looked appropriate." Sue, the student's faculty adviser, jumped into the discussion. Given Sue's institutional relationship with the student, she was probably going (and was seen by the group as going) to the student's defense.

Excerpt 125

1 Fred: . . . the idea that we're just going to look at appearances of, of being attentive and have that count as being interpersonally skilled and we're just uh

2 Sue: Well let me, let, ((group laughter)) this goes back to
the construction thing

((*loud group laughter*))

3 Sue: All I'm trying to say is what it looks like in the social
world, it's not real, people are or aren't. It seems as it's not
((said laughingly))

((*loud group laughter*))

4 Ed: I don't even know what is attacked

((*group laughter*))

5 Rob: Those, those damn rhetoricians you can't ( ) ((laughing))
argue uh, argue reality, they're opting for appearance.
Argue for appearance, they come back with reality. ((said
laughing))

6 Sue: So you take appearance and that's the way into reality.

7 Tim: You're pretty genuine right now.

((*group laugh*))

8 Sue: Well . . . [Five short exchanges between Sue and Tim]

17 Tim: . . . Now you may want to do that, you may want to say that
as a teacher of interpersonal communication I find that
distinction meaningless. But knowing you, Sue, you especially, ((laughter from group)) you couldn't make that
claim.

18 Rob: Tim Astoff seems not to be here today.

((*laughter from group*))

19 Rob: It seems to me if he were he would argue along this line.
((group laughter)) That you, that you have to view this
ironically ((group laughter)) Right? that

((*group laughter*))

20 Jesse: Evan.

21 Evan: Are you all finished?

22 Rob: Yeah, well you can fill in the rest.

((*group laughter*))

23 Evan: No seriously I think that . . .

When people share understandings about specific people's characters
and routine meanings in a situation, humor can be accomplished by saying something incongruous. In this exchange among faculty at State U,
we see people playing off each other's character and category member-
ships as well as potential incongruities between the topic and the interactional situation. I will not attempt to explicate all that made this

exchange funny to the participants, but I will highlight several features. First, the topic is a serious and central one within this academic discipline: What is the relationship between communicative appearances and what is real? Positions on this issue influence many other specific issues. This is serious talk. By referencing the issue in utterance 2 as "the construction thing" Sue uses a more colloquial and informal style[3] than is typical in this context.

Also, individual faculty members poke fun at facets of their colleagues' beliefs and interactional styles. In utterance 5, Rob's comment about those "damn rhetoricians" not only uses colloquial language but frames Fred as being part of a group that develops these contrary views. Rob's later comment about "Tim Astoff seems not be here today" is funny both because it follows a comment by Tim Astoff and because it goes on to offer a caricature of him (remarking about irony) that is recognizable to participants. In addition, Tim and Sue's community personae are at least somewhat incongruous with the positions they argue; that is, strategic Tim argues for reality, and sincere Sue argues for appearances.

Moreover, because laughter comes from everybody—the implicated parties as well as the rest of the group—the group enacts a sense of itself as a situation in which people do not take themselves too seriously. In engaging in this playful sequence at this particular juncture, the group moves away from a discussion focus that posed a threat to graduate student Jesse. In addition, the group had a moment of fun and affirmed through its actions that caring about people and being critical of them and their views were connected activities. In sum, State U managed the play/serious tension by developing an interactional climate of playful seriousness. While interactional moments sometimes went too far one way or the other, by pursuing each value the State U group enacted intellectual community.

PARTICIPATION AS OBLIGATORY VOLUNTARISM

Participation at State U's weekly colloquium was officially voluntary. No student received course credit for attending; no faculty member received teaching credit. No departmental rule existed requiring attendance for any party. Rather, colloquium at State U was conceived as a talk activity to which graduate students and faculty would come spontaneously because they cared about ideas and it served their interests to do so. Although participation was officially voluntary, many participants, and especially faculty,

---

[3.] Scotton (1985) describes this process as style shifting, and identifies a varied set of interactional functions served by it.

thought about the activity as having a strong obligation component. In response to an interview question about how colloquium could be improved, faculty member Stephen said the following:

Excerpt 126

I know it's heresy to say it. I don't think we need a weekly colloquium. I think we could be a little more every other week or something like that . . . I think there is value of course to the habit of going to the colloquium every Monday but I sometimes feel as if I oughta go even though I've gotta make ten phone calls and I've just come out of class and need to unwind.

Stephen's remark is interesting in several ways. First, in framing his comment about meeting every other week as "heresy," he implicitly marks what he takes to be the community's belief about colloquium; that weekly scheduling is sacred and not to be questioned. This is intriguing, because in many academic departments, weekly colloquium meetings, year in, year out, are undoubtedly more an exception than the rule. In offering a reason that the colloquium would be better as a biweekly event ("there is value to the habit of going but I sometimes feel as if I oughta go") Stephen identifies the importance of maintaining colloquium as a talk occasion that is freely chosen because of its intrinsic worth rather than being attended only because one "oughta go."

To accomplish a sense that participants were freely choosing, Stephen proposed having colloquia less frequently. Of note is the fact that he did not propose encouraging participants to attend sessions selectively. One reason for this was the attributional significance attached to nonattendance at State U. Colloquium attendance was seen as providing information about one's intellectual and scholarly commitments. When asked about informal purposes of colloquium, faculty member Arnold spoke to this issue:

Excerpt 127

I think it's a barometer to a certain extent of how much people are interested in research of graduate students and faculty. I think the faculty who don't come are the ones who don't do research and the graduate students who don't come are the ones who, I think, have less interest in research per se than other things.

Since attendance was not obligatory, a person's choice to attend was taken to say something about whether a person was interested and concerned about ideas and research. An upshot of this was that attendance among faculty involved with the graduate program was uniformly good. No graduate faculty member wanted to be perceived as someone who did not care about ideas and research. On the other hand, attendance from graduate students was more variable, both within a year and across years. This pattern of fluctuating involvement was seen as a problem by faculty members.

Excerpt 128

One impression I've had this year and I don't have hard data to back it up, my impression is that there are fewer graduate students coming and that concerns me. (faculty member)

In fact, a concern that too many graduate students had chosen not to attend the prior semester became the focus of a departmental memo sent by the director of graduate studies to all graduate students and faculty advisors at the start of one winter semester. This memo is quoted in full in Excerpt 129:

Excerpt 129

MEMORANDUM
      DATE: January 19, 1989
      TO: State U Graduate Students and Advisors
      FROM: Barry Street, State U Director of Graduate Studies
      RE: Colloquium

Reminder: Colloquium will be held every Monday, 2:45–4:00, in 351 [building name], beginning January 30.

All graduate students are expected to attend the colloquium regularly. Understandably, a given individual's schedule may make it impossible for that individual to participate in a given week or semester. This will most often be the case for part time students. Everyone, however, should endeavor to arrange his or her schedule to make attendance possible. If there is a reason *you* will not be able to participate this semester, I would appreciate if you would let me know. I will be asking.

Obviously I would not be writing such a memo if I were not concerned about an apparent erosion of this norm. The colloquium remains our chief means of community-building within an urban university program that is naturally subject to various centrifugal forces. Attendance was down last semester, especially among students. Jim Harris [colloquium chair] reports an underwhelming response to his memo requesting volunteers for this semester.

I've heard that some students feel the colloquium is "for" the faculty and that they (the students) have no real role. *Maybe we ought to have a colloquium to discuss that problem (N.B. Harris),* if it is a problem. My own feeling is that all students can, and many do, benefit tremendously from the experience, and that we simply must do whatever it takes to remove any impediments that stand in the way of those benefits.

PhD students are required to do one "official" colloquium presentation, but everyone, including MA students, ought to avail themselves of the opportunity to present their ideas. Will you be presenting anything at a conference this spring? Will you be submitting anything to [name of national professional association] (deadline 2/15)? Do you have a research study or independent project recently or "almost" done? Consider signing up for a colloquium presentation. You can do a "dry run" before an audience that is relatively "safe" and yet at least as critical as any you will confront anywhere. Yes you will get critical questions and comments. That's the point.

One last point. Yes the colloquium topic is often not central to your individual interests. Sometimes it's inconvenient to attend. Sometimes you do attend and it turns out to be downright dull, or obnoxious. Part of being a "good citizen" in this community is to attend every week anyway, to grant the speaker the courtesy of an audience and to make the continuation of the institution possible.

We didn't promise you a rose garden.

This memo, which State U participants came to reference as "the rose garden memo," apparently did generate an increase in graduate student attendance. The memo functions as an unmitigated directive from a key organizational member of what everyone should do; it presented the colloquium as an obligation for anyone who wished to regard self as a good citizen of the community. In essence, against a backdrop without existing official rules, it sought to insure that participants regularly chose to attend. This created a paradox that did not go unnoticed among participants. In discussing how colloquium could be improved, graduate student Eric said:

Excerpt 130

I think attitudes could be improved . . . I'm not quite sure how you improve that but just a more consistent idea of what's supposed to be done up there and people trying to carry that through as opposed to just showing up I think may be beneficial. Uh I just don't, I I see the usefulness of the aim to be there as an audience. At the same time it kinda takes away from the main purpose. That is, people concerned about knowledge. (graduate student)

Eric's comment illustrates the tension. To the degree that people feel that they must show up, experiencing the occasion as one that has been chosen because a person is "concerned about knowledge" is difficult. Yet in an environment in which people are routinely overcommitted and pressed for time, truly voluntary attendance is likely to lead to an activity's demise and the disintegration of community. State U managed this tension by treating participation as a matter of obligatory voluntarism. No one was required to attend but everyone was obligated to come voluntarily. In so doing State U maintained its balance on a tightrope; it insured that community did not fracture because of lack of participation while allowing each person to sustain some sense of personal involvement as being chosen rather than coerced.

III

Implications

10

Cultivating Better Discussion

Through listening to academics' thoughts about intellectual discussion, and studying their talking, we have come to a view of colloquium more complex than the characterization with which we started. That is, although colloquium can be an occasion when ideas advance and are tested, knowledge is produced, and truth sought, it also can be an occasion that accomplishes none of these. These valued outcomes of people talking about ideas happen only some of the time, only partially, and only when the people involved manage the problems inherent in the situation well. At multiple levels—as academic departmental groups, as discussants and presenters, as commentators after the fact—the participants find a tangled web of problems that must be confronted and managed. What are the most suitable ways to manage intellectual discussion problems? How should academic colloquia be structured? What communicative ideals should motivate people's talk? How should people talk about academic discussion situations?

In this chapter I draw together and develop more fully suggestions at which I have only hinted in earlier pages. The suggestions are crystallized as three proposals, each offered from a different vantage point. The first proposal is addressed to academic groups as they consider how to design colloquia; the second describes the interactional ideal I would advise individuals to pursue; the third offers a policy for how academics should talk about colloquia in which they have participated. In developing each proposal, I move back and forth between practical suggestions and moral principles, ideals for action and concrete communicative techniques. I do so in the belief that cultivating a practice must attend simultaneously to questions of why something should be done and of how it could be done.

PROPOSAL 1: ACADEMIC GROUPS SHOULD GIVE ONGOING ATTENTION TO MAINTAINING A STRONG SENSE OF INTELLECTUAL COMMUNITY WITHIN THE GROUP

Chapters 6 and 8 identified a range of problems confronting academic colloquia. Among these problems were a group's need to avoid overly heated and hostile exchanges while ensuring that boring discussions were not tacitly promoted; to create an appropriately playful/serious environment that did not tilt too far in either direction; to make certain that the discussion became neither a social chitchat nor a lecture from a knowledgeable to ignorants; and to reconcile the contradictory injunctions about how experience/status differences should be managed. These problems will be minimized if academic groups attend to developing intellectual community. While building and sustaining intellectual community is a reasonable end goal for a group—as it was at State U—it is also the essential condition for a group's routine accomplishment of good discussion.

Intellectual community exists when a group shares a commitment to a set of issues and respects and supports each member in voicing disagreement and expressing criticism about positions bearing on those issues. Intellectual community, as noted in the previous chapter, is an ideal, a state that can be approached to different degrees but never is realized fully. The closer a group approaches the ideal, the better its routine intellectual discussions will be.

Creating a sense of community is the primary way groups minimize the seriousness of the dangers to good discussion. When people feel comfortable in a group and generally feel respected, they are most willing to express ideas that may generate feelings. When a respectful group climate has been established, participants will be the least fearful that what they say will be taken wrong. Participants can criticize another's idea strongly without worry that the other will see them as personally hostile. At the same time, in a community, participants will be more willing to risk saying something that could reflect negatively on the self. When people feel appreciated and respected by others, they are considerably less threatened by the knowledge that they have uttered something stupid on a particular occasion. Establishing intellectual community, then, minimizes the dangers that the discussion will be boring and lifeless because feelings are suppressed. It also minimizes the danger that expression of feelings will be interpreted (and intended) as personal attack or defensiveness.

Similarly, the danger of discussion turning into a series of long-winded monologues, generally more serious than the danger of lively expressions of ignorance, is considerably smaller when a group has established a strong sense of intellectual community. When concerns about how others will assess self are unduly high—people know each other in limited ways (as an intellectual position) or not at all—discussants are most likely to preplan extensive comments designed to display their intellectual competence. The goodwill and sense of trust that a sense of community make salient enables the kind of think-aloud talk that is typically shorter and more engaged with what was previously said. Also, when individuals experience themselves as a community, they are more likely to feel responsible to the group, to show their investment through participation, and at the same time to avoid dominating the talk.

Proposing that academic groups seek to establish themselves as intellectual communities in order to cultivate good discussion is unlikely to be controversial, but interactively accomplishing this state of affairs will challenge most academic groups. As suggested in the previous chapter, intellectual community is a fragile state, one that can be disabled or even destroyed by seemingly reasonable actions taken to address an identified problem. Usually the problem is but one side of a precarious tension in which the other side is less visible to the group.

An intellectual community is a set of people who perceive themselves to be a group: Members are committed to each other. It is also a collection of individuals who come together because of similar intellectual interests. At a practical level, an interactional problem revolves around ensuring sufficiently consistent participation that a set of people perceive themselves to be a group, while simultaneously promoting a sense that attendance is an act freely chosen out of interest in, and commitment to, a set of issues. State U managed this tension reasonably well through its cultivation of obligatory voluntarism. Other groups about which interviewees spoke, or ones in which I myself have participated, have managed this tension less well, falling prey to one or another excess.

On the one hand, academic groups require attendance in ways that lead individuals to see the departmental colloquium as an institutional requirement for which an academic's interest is an irrelevant consideration. That is, colloquium is a bureaucratic requirement of departmental life. Or on the other hand, academics in a group see themselves as coming together out of shared interests, but, as one interviewee recounted about a past group experience among a small set of people, the group "fizzled after a fairly short time."

If a voluntarily formed colloquium is drawing from a large enough participant group, it probably will not die off quickly, but it will have another problem. If people come voluntarily when it interests them, then different people are likely to be there on different occasions. That is, no consistent group of people will be participating. In such a colloquium, the group is more likely to experience itself as an audience than as a community. Large colloquium groups with a norm of voluntary participation have an additional consequence; they cannot avoid being an identity threat to a colloquium presenter. Each colloquium occasion becomes viewable as a reading of a presenter's standing in the departmental group. If a lot of people show up, the presenter can infer that he or she is regarded as intellectually interesting, or at least as an important person. If few people show up, the presenter might easily infer that he or she is regarded as intellectually uninteresting or someone who can be offended without consequences.

In managing the tension surrounding the creation of a group that comes out of interest, departments should frame colloquium situations in ways that simultaneously highlight their obligatory and voluntary nature (or conversely, downplay both), recognizing the paradoxical nature of that injunction. For instance, besides the strategy State U used to manage the tension, a department group could make attendance obligatory (students receive course credit for participating; faculty hold each other accountable for attending) while engaging in moves that de-emphasize the degree of obligation (meet every several weeks, make the amount of credit assigned minimal, make formal evaluation a secondary concern by treating grading as pass/fail). In addition, an academic department could structure the occasion in ways that draw upon the practices of more voluntary occasions (i.e., meet in people's homes, meet over lunch, meet in the evenings or on Sunday, have refreshments, and so on).

Two other practical issues have a strong effect on a group's ability to create and sustain intellectual community: the typical group size and the pattern of institutional ranks among regular participants. Fostering of intellectual community, I suggest, will be aided when a group has at least 7 to 8 people and no more than 25 or 30, with 10 to 20 participants being optimal. For community to be meaningful, it needs to involve more than a handful of like-minded people who spend time with each other informally. That is, semipublic occasions, such as discussion groups, that involve a larger number of people are generally seen as more important than those which attract only a few. Thus, the seriousness of an intellectual community's enterprise is underscored by its size. At the same time, intellectual community is a special type of community, one in which there is a commitment to people talking with each other about ideas. To realize this commitment, even in a partial, imperfect way, necessitates that the group size not be too large. If large numbers of participants feel that they are no more than audience, and could not speak if they wanted to, intellectual community will not be realized.

Practical problems in achieving an optimal size arise when disparities exist between obvious division lines in a department or interdisciplinary unit and the numbers of people implicated by a particular division. For instance, a colloquium group could include a whole department, could be composed of everyone interested in a certain broad area, or could include only persons of a certain rank (just students or just faculty). Each of these divisions could be highly suitable or problematic. If drawing the boundary is problematic by virtue of marking off either too few or too many people, then the group needs to weigh the effects of its less than optimal size against the possible effects of whatever actions would be required to achieve an optimal group size. Often, the effects of actions taken to achieve optimal size may well be more negative than those of continuing to operate at a less than optimal size.

The other practical problem that can influence a group's ability to create community is the institutional rank composition of its members. During the year I participated in and observed the University X colloquium—a colloquium open to all departmental members—there was consistent attendance and participation from first-year doctoral students and senior faculty. Advanced graduate students were almost never there and junior faculty attendance, while better, was sporadic. The upshot of this was a colloquium group in which there often were no people of moderate experience and middle rank. A participant was either a complete novice (first-year graduate student) or a highly experienced academic (tenured faculty member). In such a group, tensions between recognizing experience differences and considering ideas on their merit seemed unreconcilable. A discussion participant could do one or the other, but not both. As a result, discussions tended to be strained, to turn into tutorials, or to be conducted entirely among faculty participants. In addition, beginning graduate students had no models to represent the kind of verbal engagement they could expect as they spent more time in the community.

In terms of a group's rank composition, then, I would recommend that a group be relatively homogeneous in rank (i.e., all graduate students or all faculty) or status inclusive. A status inclusive group is one that includes a reasonable number of participants of all ranks represented in the academic unit—beginning graduate students, advanced graduate students, junior faculty, and senior faculty. A status-inclusive group will not eliminate tensions between considering ideas on their merit or in terms of the experience level of the other, but such a group composition will facilitate the display of the full range of communicative practices that can be used in responding to the experience/merit dilemma. Such display is the best way to validate the importance of taking seriously both parts of the tension. Moreover, status-inclusive groups accomplish the task of socializing students to an academic discipline, an important additional goal of many colloquium groups.

In sum, to promote good discussion, academic groups should seek to structure themselves in ways that will facilitate a sense of intellectual community. This means giving attention to structural issues such as the size of the group, its status composition, and the ways in which participation/attendance is to be encouraged or regulated. Besides these structural features, good discussion requires individual participants to talk with each other in certain ways.

PROPOSAL 2: ACADEMIC PARTICIPANTS SHOULD PURSUE A DILEMMATIC IDEAL, RECOGNIZING THAT DISCUSSION MUST BE THOUGHT OF AS BOTH DIALECTIC AND CONSTRUCTIVE CRITICISM.

When people describe problems in a situation, their descriptions imply what they take to be solutions. That is, descriptions routinely convey evaluative loadings—someone or something is praised or blamed—therein cuing what ideal a person holds. From interviews at State U and University X, two ideals can be reconstructed from participants' analyses of problems. A first ideal was that academic discussion should be conceived of as dialectic. In dialectic, the central purpose of discussion is the critique of ideas; opposition and disagreement are necessary parts of the process, and participants are expected to pursue critique in whatever avenue discussion makes relevant. A person who disagrees with an idea, or even is repulsed by it, has a right to express that reaction. Within the dialectic ideal, ideas are important, and passion about them is a desirable feature of intellectual discussion. Ideas that are wrongheaded, evil, or harmful should be responded to with strong feeling. Moreover, in the pursuit of ideas, a participant's status should be irrelevant to how ideas are talked about. The ideas of a speaker with stature in academe should not be entitled to uncritical acceptance.

The second ideal conceives of intellectual discussion as constructive criticism. Within this view, intellectual discussion is a talk designed to build upon, and shape, individual community members' ideas in a positive and supportive manner. While idea critique is important, constructive criticism recognizes the legitimacy of constraints on expression. Constructive criticism takes seriously the idea that not everything a person thinks should be said. It is the critic's responsibility to consider what criticisms will be helpful rather than harmful to a participant in the discussion situation. Similarly, the conception of intellectual discussion as construction suggests that the foundation provided is worthy and that the discussant's task is to figure out ways to help the builder develop an intellectual structure on the selected ground. Moreover, in recognizing that people are tied emotionally to the ideas that they espouse, constructive criticism assumes the discussants have a responsibility to temper the expression of their feelings in ways that show respect and avoid the possibility of humiliating a person to whom it is directed.[1]

These two ideals of discussion were not equally valued and viable notions of "the good." Rather, discussion as dialectic was the dominant ideal, and constructive criticism was the challenger. Dialectic's dominance (and constructive criticism's challenger status) is suggested by two different kinds of evidence. First, the responses interviewees gave to explicit questions about definitions and purposes of intellectual discussion corresponded (or gave more weight) to the dialectic ideal. For instance, in response to an interview question that asked participants at University X what intellectual discussion was, two faculty members who favored different ideals said the following:

Excerpt 131

Sandy [interviewer's name] ((laugh)) having to do with ideas of course. And it's theory based for me. (University X)

Excerpt 132

Two or more people, uh, focusing on ideas . . . I'd include, you know, when defenses go well for dissertation and things like that. I'd say the ideal that should be is an intellectual discussion, assuming the work has been done and it's been done well, that everybody can sit there and explore ideas and get excited about things. Uh so I guess the common commitment is to ideas. *And then related is like, well, well I guess, parallel at the same time, a commitment to respecting one another* in the discussion and recognizing there may be big differences. (University X)

By saying the interviewer's name, laughing, and following a very brief definition with the phrase "of course," faculty member Jan (Excerpt 131) conveys her sense that she is stating the obvious, responding to a question that nobody would answer differently. Her answer never mentions people and the relationships they should seek to have with each other. Anton's answer (Excerpt 132) points to a different view of intellectual discussion. From its opening, his response puts people into the activity, "two or more people focusing on ideas," but even in his more person-friendly definition,

---

[1] Katriel (1986) describes differences between Israelis and Americans as involving this difference between a speaker's right to be expressive and a listener's right to have his or her feelings protected. A similar distinction is made by Kochman (1981) for Black and white Americans.

the dominant emphasis is on idea exploration. Anton's hesitant after-thought, "And then related is like, well, well I guess, parallel at the same time," confirms the salience of dialectic rather than overturning it. Put somewhat differently, the sheer conversational struggling he exhibits as he claims that intellectual discussion is committed to "respecting one another" suggests constructive criticism's lesser obviousness and taken-for-granted status.

A second kind of evidence that points to the dominant status of the dialectic ideal was its markedly more frequent use as the implicit comparison point—the assumed way things are—when people argued for the way intellectual discussion should be. Of note was the relative rarity of comparison in the other direction: people arguing for dialectic where constructive criticism was the implicit assumption about how discussion routinely operated. In arguing for constructive criticism, people did not merely represent the dialectic view neutrally. Instead, they characterized it in ways that trivialized it, suggested its unreasonableness, and portrayed it negatively. Consider the following two excerpts from Zelda, a junior faculty member at University X:

Excerpt 133

[in response to a question about what she liked least about the departmental colloquium]
    There's another thing that I don't like because I'm not comfortable with it, would be conversations that occur more from what I call, uh, debate-oriented tradition where uh, where we take everything, we take an idea and *we tear it apart.* We say what isn't relevant to us because of the research method, or because the idea wasn't stimulating or interesting, or *because of some quirk that any of us might have.* That almost becomes the contest in itself, to see if you can come up with things that you don't like about this.

Excerpt 134

[in response to a question about the role of criticism]
    I'm not anticritical, I just see criticism helping, for me, for my style, healthy criticism . . . breaking something down into its various parts so that I can really understand it. That is different than seeing "criticism of" . . . When I was a graduate student I'd really feel shot down if somebody told me I had to *dot my i.* But you know I see a legitimate place for criticism that would talk about dotting my i. But what if they just stop at that? And if I don't work with the soil of the idea that the person is working with in their head, I've missed it as a teacher. And as a participant in intellectual discussion.

Zelda's comments imply a strong constructionist view of what intellectual criticism should be about as well as a negative attitude toward what she portrays as the common practice of focusing on ideas. From her perspective, the typical focus on ideas is "tearing them apart," or challenging them for reasons that are personalized matters of taste or highly idiosyncratic "the idea wasn't stimulating or interesting, or because of some quirk that any of us might have." Disagreeing with someone is characterized as telling people how to "dot their i's." In contrast, Zelda's view of good discussion is not "anticritical" but "work[ing] with the soil of the idea that the person is working with in their head"; it is the discussant taking a presenter's purposes seriously in figuring out what to say.

Such a view, albeit recognizing more difficulties in adequately diagnosing when someone has been constructive, is echoed by junior faculty member Lester from State U when he discusses the kind of responses he hopes for when he is a presenter.

Excerpt 135

Constructive criticism. And what I mean by that is uhm, I'm looking for, I'm hoping that uhm people will try to think along with me, uhm and take into account what, what my purposes are, what I'm trying to do, uhm in the research that I'm talking about. Uhm point out weaknesses in the argument, places where it doesn't hold together, hold together, well, um other things that I could look at that would be helpful . . . *To some extent criticize my assumptions* ah if they think I'm making some assumptions that they find problematic. I think it's good for them to point that out. There's a fine line, uh I'm not sure how to explain exactly, but there's a fine line between pointing out assumptions somebody's making and ask-, and asking do you accept this and why? . . . Sometimes that ends up moving you away from trying to think along with the person, uhm you know what happens is that sometimes, people will lis-, will read an article or *will listen to a presentation and they think about it completely within uhm the assumptions they make in their research and what their interests and concerns. And any comments that they make are completely from within that perspective.* Ah, it's good to be aware of how what you're doing looks from other perspectives but uh especially if you get involved in any long dialogue, it's important for it not just to be from that other person's point of view without their making any effort to move beyond it.

In imagining himself in the presenter's position, Lester argues for a nuanced version of a constructive criticism ideal. It is nuanced in that it works to grant legitimacy to certain parts of the dialectic view of discussion even while arguing for the superiority of constructive criticism. Criticizing intellectual foundations, a presenter's starting assumptions is acceptable "to some extent." According to Lester, the extent would be the degree to which that kind of foundational criticism helps presenters and avoids moving them away from their central intellectual goals. This criterion is the fundamental difference in conceiving of intellectual discussion as constructive criticism rather than dialectic. Of interest is the way Lester implies that the opposite of constructive criticism involves intellectual narrowness. In describing the alternative as "comments completely within that perspective" and failing to make "any effort to move beyond it [the person's position]." Lester implies that pursuing issues that are not consonant with a presenter's focus are undesirable and inappropriate.

Another belief about which participants held varied views was the relational dimension that was to be privileged. Psychologists and communication scholars have long suggested that relationships involve two central dimensions: solidarity and power.[2] In looking at the intellectual discussion situation, people tended to privilege one of these dimensions and downplay or ignore the other. Some participants tended to emphasize the importance of minimizing status differences. From this viewpoint, discussants needed to be cautious about positivity, because it easily could become a device to further inequality among participants. This conception is reflected in the comment from a senior faculty member (Excerpt 67) who highlighted how praise was often patronizing. In contrast, other interviewees expressed more concern about the harm caused to people by comments that engendered negative feelings about self and work. In response to a probe about whether criticism could have negative potential, Mary, a junior faculty member at University X, said that criticism:

Excerpt 136

shouldn't uh make people question their basic abilities because uh everybody, I think everybody can engage in intellectual discussion. There's no reason to turn anybody off from it, from engaging ideas to make the other person feel bad, look bad. Uhm and criticizing fine points of things that really aren't that important and make people discouraged about their work because it's not perfect, when nobody's work's perfect.

Mary's comment links people "question[ing] their basic abilities" with "criticizing fine points of things that really aren't that important." In lining up these two activities so unproblematically—questioning basic abilities and nitpicking—Mary conveys a strong negative evaluation of discussants who make comments that lead people seriously to doubt their intellectual ability.

Unsurprisingly, preference for avoiding one relational excess or the other was not random but rather tended to link with other beliefs. In particular, a

---

2. Cappella and Street (1985) review this literature.

concern to minimize the impact of rank differences tended to be displayed with the expectation that intellectual discussion would focus on ideas, that exploration of ideas would be guided by all parties' interests (not just those of the presenter), and that passion about ideas was legitimate. In contrast, the expectation that people should be sensitive to rank differences and edit negative expressions that might wound others tended to co-occur with the expectation that intellectual discussion was talk between people, and that idea exploration should be constrained by what would be helpful to the person presenting the ideas.

While individual participants tended to favor one or the other ideal, almost all interviewees made comments sympathetic to both ideals. For instance, junior faculty member Lynn had responded to a question about the role of praise in intellectual discussion this way:

Excerpt 137

If you define praise as reinforcing people for ideas, uh then I would say none.

Such an evaluation is consistent with the dialectical position that defines intellectual discussion as talk about ideas, a position Lynn took over much of the interview. Nonetheless, when the focus of the interview was on expected discussion differences in situations where one person presented his or her work versus discussing a common reading, Lynn argued for the importance of praising.

Excerpt 138

You discuss the ideas in a way that allows the person to save face . . . it's also important to do praising at some point. It was a good paper and an interesting argument. Or what a well par-, well-crafted paragraph. Because there is so much at stake in presenting your own work that the absence of praise would be noticed even, even if it's perfunctory.

In Lynn's second comment, she is much more focused on the fact that intellectual discussion is talk between people; in framing it as talk between people, the constructive criticism ideal becomes salient. Similarly, Lester (Excerpt 135), who made the nuanced case for constructive criticism, argued elsewhere about the demands of "intellectual integrity," a sentiment more consonant with a dialectic ideal (see Excerpt 21).

Thus far, I have articulated two different solutions to the problems of intellectual discussion. These solutions are reconstructions of the normative beliefs a set of academics held about good intellectual discussion. I label these reconstructions *situated ideals* to capture their character as philosophical positions that arise, not abstractly, but out of the particulars of this communicative practice. These situated ideals provide an especially good place to begin thinking about how people ought to talk with each other. Because they are sensitive to the problems and choice points that actors actually face as they do intellectual discussion, they are likely to be implicative for action. Some questions arise, however: How do we get from these two competing ideals to a proposal? Is one ideal to be preferred? Can the tensions between dialectic and constructive criticism be resolved in a new transcendent ideal? Should the two ideals be understood as horns of a dilemma?

I propose that the two situated ideals be understood as opposing horns of an existential dilemma, a dilemma inherent in the practice of intellectual discussion that cannot be resolved but can be managed more or less well. The close coupling of people and ideas involved in intellectual discussion is the fundamental feature of this communicative activity. Intellectual discussion *is* talk between people about ideas; ideas and people cannot and should not be separated. Colloquium, as one participant said, is a "dance of ideas and personalities."

To pursue a dilemmatic ideal that assumes intellectual discussion must be constituted as both dialectic and constructive criticism is to recognize that certain tensions are intrinsic to intellectual discussion. When people discuss ideas that are personally important to them, they are implicated in emotionally serious, and reputationally significant, ways. As a result, discussion participants cannot escape conflicts in which communicative actions may produce undesirable outcomes. Unrestrained pursuit of the dialectic ideal may injure people and relationships and may rend the social fabric without which intellectual discussion becomes impossible. If the expression of ideas is dictated primarily by concerns about personal and relational needs, however, discussion will degenerate into therapy and will render unlikely the intellectual growth that constructive criticism ideally fosters. Moral demands of intellectual integrity on the one hand, and responsibility to persons on the other, are sometimes such that intellectual discussion becomes impossible and must be suspended. Integrity, for example, might require that something must be said regardless of the social consequences, or concern for a person might require that something not be said regardless of its truth. Quite often, however, the exercise of good judgment as one pursues the dilemmatic ideal of constructive criticism and dialectic, when coupled with the use of conversational techniques that are situationally appropriate, will enable communicators to continue discussion in productive ways.

Earlier chapters described the conversational techniques used by academics: (a) to position speakers and others in relation to the ideas under discussion, (b) to account for potentially disputable choices, (c) to enact institutional relationships, (d) to challenge (or support) ideas/persons in straightforward, subtle, or mitigated fashion, and (e) to create a supportive and playful serious climate. Each of the identified techniques can enhance, but also could damage, discussion quality. To facilitate high quality discussion, academics guided by the dilemmatic ideal will need to reflect about potential conversational moves in light of a situation's particular problems. This reflection process will be most useful for shaping future practice if it extends to the postmortem conversations academics have in hallways and offices. That is, it is likely to be in individuals' after-the-fact reflections, when done thoughtfully, that ways of responding more appropriately for the next heated (or boring) discussion moment will be created or rediscovered.

PROPOSAL 3: ACADEMICS SHOULD (A) TALK ABOUT COLLOQUIA IN WAYS THAT RECOGNIZE THE POSITIONED NATURE OF PROBLEM ANALYSES, AND (B) USE LANGUAGE PRACTICES THAT KEEP THE DILEMMATIC CHARACTER OF ACADEMIC COLLOQUIA VISIBLE.

In this book, the problems of academic colloquia have been considered from multiple perspectives: the group, presenters and discussants, and faculty and graduate students. Colloquium problems, I have attempted to show, do not comprise a fixed set, but change character and seriousness depending on the perspective taken. Stated simply, problem analyses are positioned. What an academic takes to be "the problem" will be shaped by an academic's place in the setting. This notion of problem analyses being positioned is particularly implicative for academics in their roles as faculty and as graduate students. The assertion that faculty and graduate students are often critical of each other's communicative actions is one with which few would disagree. What I regard as less well acknowledged is the forceful way institutional position shapes the formulation of colloquium problems such that blame will be assigned freely to the other, and responsibility stingily given to self.

By and large, I would argue, faculty members fail to recognize the full array of ways in which higher institutional rank privileges them and creates disadvantages for graduate students. Because most faculty members are confident that they do not, or would not, abuse power, they presuppose that in a situation in which they speak, the merit of what is being discussed is the only issue. While other faculty may not succeed, they as individuals have left rank at the colloquium door. Thus, if graduate students are not speaking out much, or persuasively, it can only be because students possess intellectual deficiencies, have problems of being shy, or are uncomfortable in making verbal arguments. At its baldest, faculty members are much too likely to assign the difficulties experienced in having good discussion to the supposed fact that the particular group of students participating in a departmental colloquium is of less than superior quality.

In contrast, graduate students, in their analyses of colloquium problems, fail to take themselves seriously as intellectuals and colloquium contributors. Faculty are presupposed to be doing no more than playing power games in which students are pawns; criticism of student ideas is a play in an academic political game that has little to do with the intellectual quality of a student's work. Crudely put, students are all too likely to assign themselves the role of victim and to blame poor discussion quality on faculty who engage in arbitrary expressions of power.

Admittedly these portraits of the views of typical colloquia problems are caricatures. Interviewees of all ranks accepted a greater amount of personal responsibility and saw the situation with more complexity than is captured in each portrait. Although not accurate in any strict sense, the portraits, I would suggest, capture a truth about an academic's likely bias in analyzing discussion situations. Faculty members underestimate the role of their own power; graduate students overestimate the contribution of power differences. To rectify this positioning bias, I propose that faculty members query carefully the ways in which they use their own institutional status to get what they want, and work to identify the subtle ways rank is shaping what can and cannot happen in the situation. At the same time, graduate students need to recognize their own agency in intellectual discussions and to take responsibility for shaping discussion.

In addition to increased sensitivity to the consequences of positioning, increased sensitivity to routine language use might improve academics' experiences of colloquia. Several years ago, I presented some of the ideas in this book to a departmental colloquium. Eric, a faculty member, remarked only half-jokingly that the problem would be solved if every person had to wear a paper bag over his or her head. This remark, made in the context of other discussant remarks about the pretentiousness, intellectual posturing, and deference needs frequently exhibited by senior faculty, sought to make all discussants equal. Presumably masking would prevent special privileges for those with high institutional status. Such a condition would allow the good ideas of institutionally junior people to receive the accord that they should get but often did not because of the corrosive influence of power relations.

Creating equality through anonymity is a good idea if the main interactional problem is that ideas are not being examined on their own merits. If, however, there is an equally serious problem of inexperienced participants being criticized too harshly, the paper bag solution will not do. Certain paper bags will be offering thoughtful, interesting, and developed ideas; others will be offering naïve or ill-informed ones. Moreover, while both good and bad ideas will be offered by people of all institutional ranks, the frequency of good ideas is likely to differ across ranks. Returning to the paper bag solution, to criticize a bag that speaks with but one year's experience in the same way as one criticizes the bag with twenty years' experience seems unfair. In talking about intellectual discussion, Eric drew upon a simple problem-solution frame. His linguistic framing made invisible other cooccurring problems that needed to be considered in seeking to develop wise solutions.

A similar problem is evidenced in Kenneth Gergen's (1994) analysis of "the limits of pure critique." After identifying five difficulties in routine critical engagement, he poses the following as the fundamental question that requires a good answer if the critical process is to be transformed: "In what sense could we remove from the field the emphasis on ego, the sense of authorial ownership of arguments, and threat of spoiled identities?" (p. 73).

Like Eric's paper bag comment, Gergen's analysis presupposes a straightforward problem: People are too closely coupled to their ideas. Framing the problem of critical discussion as requiring people to minimize emotional investment in ideas is but half of the difficulty. Without attention to the cooccurring problem of the need to avoid wooden, abstracted, and depersonalized discussions that bore everyone, Gergen's solution is likely to kill what is most valued about this form of talk. Drawing upon a dilemmatic frame whenever colloquium occasions are discussed would promote better quality discussions in two ways.

First, when academics' linguistic formulations routinely recognize the precarious tensions involved in accomplishing good discussion, there is likely to be greater enjoyment when the discussion goes well and less intolerance when the discussion goes too far one way or the other. For most people, accomplishing a difficult task is more rewarding than accomplishing an easy one. Thus, if academics talk about intellectual discussion using analogies and linguistic frames that recognize its difficulty, they are likely to feel more satisfaction when it unfolds well. Too, when problems occur, a recognition of the inherent delicacy of the needed balancing act is likely to make participants more understanding of each other's failures. At the same time, the fostering of more tolerant attitudes should increase a group's sense of itself as an intellectual community, a state that in turn should further facilitate good discussion.

Second, if people routinely talk about an occasion in ways that recognize the actual character of difficulties that communicators face, they are more likely to generate novel conversational strategies that are better responses to situational problems. That is, appropriate new conversational techniques are most likely to emerge as people discuss a practice using dilemma-sensitive analogies.

The claim that the language people use to talk about the world affects how they understand it is an old one.[3] I would apply this commonplace to the academic colloquium to suggest that dilemma-sensitive linguistic formulations are what is needed. Dilemma-sensitive formulations could be accomplished by routinely talking about problems as tensions. In addition, new analogies could be used for the intellectual discussion process that make visible important features. For instance, consider what would be entailed if academics talked about intellectual discussion as a golf game or compared the task of having a good discussion to the task of developing a healthy forest through using fire appropriately.

One distinctive feature about golf compared to other sports is that it allows players of widely different ability levels to play together and enjoy themselves. The game includes a handicapping system that acknowledges both individuals' ability differences, and the fact that over time individual ability levels change. Academic colloquia differ from golf in many important ways, but as with golf, discussions are likely to be most satisfying if discussion techniques are created that ensure that novice players are not stomped on, and experts are not required to play down their abilities.

Similarly, conceiving of the role of emotion in intellectual discussion as analogous to the role of fire in forest cultivation seems an especially apt metaphor. Fires destroy forests. But, as environmentalists are increasingly recognizing, fires are natural phenomena that when controlled appropriately promote the plant and animal diversity essential to a forest's continued good health. Strategically engaging in burning is good for the forest if the weather conditions are suitable. Assuming no high winds and moist surrounding terrain, a controlled fire may be exactly what is needed. Just as trying to stamp out forest fires is neither possible nor desirable, the same is true of emotion in intellectual discussion. It is not the presence of emotion that threatens good discussion but its expression in inappropriate ways. Emotion is absolutely essential to good intellectual discussion. As graduate student Elise noted in a final unsolicited comment about the State U colloquium:

Excerpt 139

I have seen, uhm, people get excited and angry, uhm, and indignant about their work, or other people's work and what they feel is important. I like seeing that—the personally invested scholar.

[3.] For instance, see Burke (1966), Sapir (1949), Lakoff and Johnson (1980), and Whorf (1956).

In sum, if academics talked about academic colloquia in language that conceptualized the activity as involving recurrent tensions, the chances of having better discussions would be increased.

WHOSE PRACTICES HAVE BEEN DESCRIBED? TO WHOM ARE THESE PROPOSALS ADDRESSED?

In a recently published interview with Erving Goffman that was conducted more than a decade earlier (Verhoeven, 1993), Goffman was asked if the ideas about which he had written in his many books were restricted to American society. Goffman, the father of detailed observation of ordinary interaction, responded:

> While I've got no grounds for describing the perimeters, the outside boundaries of the conduct that I talk about—it's usually broader than a small section of the middle class in America. I hedge my bets by saying that I'm only talking about that group. But that's just a verbal device. No one really knows the boundaries of these things .(p. 325)

I do not know the boundaries of the academic discussion processes I have characterized in this book. I expect them to apply beyond the disciplinary and geographic groups studied, but how far beyond remains to be assessed. In a spirit of tentativeness, I offer the following as likely boundaries.

First, it must be acknowledged that the conceptions of knowledge, persons, and relationships developed in this book are deeply Western, and, perhaps, particularly American. In Asian and other non-Western societies where hierarchical relations are relatively comfortable, respect for rank is important, and the need to acknowledge individual autonomy less pressing, it seems possible that the descriptions of academic discussion may not apply, and that the proposals for the cultivation of good discussion may be unsuitable.

Second, it would be surprising indeed, and counter to what scholars studying academic disciplines have noted (Bazerman & Paradis, 1991; Becher, 1989; Dillon, 1991), to find no disciplinary differences in academic colloquia. We know, for instance, that journal articles written by humanists, social scientists, and natural scientists use distinctly different authorial styles: Natural scientists downplay their personal investment in the knowledge claims, social scientists argue, and humanists seeks to make their claim and its written expression unique (Bazerman, 1988). Nevertheless, while departmental groups are expected to exhibit noticeable differences in their patterns of communication, they are expected to struggle with the colloquium dilemmas that have been described, as well as using many of the conversational practices. Put another way, distinctive styles result from how a group resolves the myriad sets of tensions: between being suitably theoretical and appropriately practical, between pursuing linguistic articulateness and interactional naturalness, between promoting a climate that insures pointed, critical engagement versus a nonthreatening one, and so on.

Whether the dilemmas are as salient in professionally linked disciplines such as law, business, education, or social work, I am uncertain. My own experience suggests that professionally linked disciplines frame more interactive situations between faculty and graduate students as occasions in which novices are expected to learn what professionals already know. That is, intellectual discussion is not the dominant frame. To the extent that my experience is representative, these proposals about colloquium talk will be applicable in only marginal ways.

Finally, the ways in which the interactional dilemmas have been framed reflect characteristic features of the discussion situation that has been focal in this book. Although different kinds of intellectual discussions have been examined, the central focus has been on research colloquia in academic departments. In this situation, the centrality of status differences and the facts that participants have ongoing day-to day relationships with each other, and that departments have the explicit mission of training and socializing graduate students, undoubtedly have shaped the dilemmas and discourse practices noted. If intellectual discussion in other academic contexts were studied—for example, seminars or symposia organized by universities or professional associations—the key interactional problems are likely to shift.

In an interdisciplinary faculty seminar within a university, for instance, we might expect participants to view their own participation as being used by the seminar participants to assess the quality of the academic departments and disciplines that other participants represent. The fact that academics are both unique intellectuals and representatives of academic disciplines in institutions where there is competition for scarce resources is likely to generate distinct interactional problems, novel communicative techniques, and perhaps even distinct situated ideals. Moreover, in discussion groups where all members are relatively equidistant from the ideas, rather than where one member is highly associated with them (as evidenced in these research colloquia), other problems are likely to become more prominent.

In this book I have demonstrated the value of a dilemmatic frame to understand the academic colloquium. I have shown that the everyday explanation that frames problems as arising because of flaws of individual personalities is inadequate. Some problems of colloquium do arise because academics are only human—emotional, concerned about status, seeking to make positive impressions. Equally serious problems arise, however, because participants are not human enough—not sufficiently passionate, attentive to expertise differences, or sensitive to legitimate worries each person has about how others view him or her. Problems of colloquium are deeply dilemmatic. At every turn, participants are confronted with interactive tensions, paradoxes, and outright contradictions. Given the pervasiveness of dilemmatic problems, a dilemmatic frame is essential for generating wise proposals for the improvment of practice and for understanding the particulars of talk. In the next and final chapter, I move beyond the colloquium to examine practical, theoretical, and philosophical issues raised by this study of the academic colloquium.

11

Epilogue

It's 2:30 Monday afternoon in the State U communication department. The weekly colloquium has begun. At today's session, the group is departing from its routine presentation format to discuss *Colloquium: Dilemmas of Academic Discourse*. In preparation for discussion, participants have been asked to think about three issues: (a) Would *Colloquium*'s model of inquiry be useful in other domains? (b) What implications are there for future communication theorizing? (c) Would reading this book improve how academics routinely conduct themselves in colloquium and related activities? I conclude by providing a transcript[1] of the group discussion.

A MODEL FOR FUTURE INQUIRY?

Rachel: Let me get the discussion going by relating the book to my own inquiry attempts. As most of you know, the last month or so I've been struggling—and I mean struggling—to conceptualize my dissertation study. In reading *Colloquium*, it occurred to me why I'm having such a difficult time. I'm betwixt and between intellectual worlds. On the one hand,

---

[1.] This colloquium conversation was created to highlight the theoretical, methodological and practical implications of this colloquium study. Because the chapter's goal is to focus readers' attention on the content of discussants' comments, I have left out the repairs, repetitions, and nonfluencies that would be present in an actual conversation. In constructing the conversation I have sought to capture criticisms that earlier readers and listeners have offered. Admittedly, though, the participants espousing the value of the book—how intellectually and practically implicative it is—have been given louder voices.

I want my research to be practical; I want to speak to a consequential problem about communication in health care
settings. At the same time, I want to do work that is deemed
high quality and advancing theory. When I think about
doing a dissertation that advances theory, I begin with existing theories, theories of teamwork and small group
processes, conflict processes, patient compliance, and so
on. When I start that way, I get stuck. I don't know how to
relate these neat explanatory theories to the problems I've
observed at St. Francis. To the extent that I've gotten close
to identifying a theoretical issue, I've abandoned my concern to do something that's likely to be helpful. So,
grounded practical theory has opened up my sense of "theory." I can take seriously the problems that nurses, physi-
cians, and all the varied kinds of therapists have as they
work with patients and each other. And, attempting to capture the character of those problems is a theoretically legitimate activity. I don't have to abandon practice as a start for
theory.

Frank: You're implying that traditional social science research
doesn't have practical implications and I don't think that's
true.

Reid: Let me jump in here. I partly agree with both of you. You
know that phrase from Kurt Lewin that's always trotted out
in discussions like this one. "There's nothing so practical as
a good theory." I agree that can be true; Lewin's work is a
nice example. But it's also the case that it's too often not
true. There was an article by Murray Davis written back in
the early seventies where he talked about what made social
science theories interesting.[2] He's a sociologist so he
focused on the theories of sociology—Marx, Weber, Mead,
those kinds of guys, but I think his point is applicable to all
of us. He argued that a primary problem with most research
was that being interesting was not systematically pursued.
The end result was that most research in the social sciences
is incredibly boring. He went on to argue that there would
be more Marx-level research, if researchers deliberately
thought about what makes a theory interesting. If in addition to trying to make our work methodologically sound, we
also sought to ask and answer interesting questions, then we

[2.] See the essay "'That's interesting!' Toward a phenomenology of sociology and a sociology of phenomenonolgy" (Davis, 1971).

more frequently would do interesting work. I think it's the same way with practical research. It's not that having implications for practice is regarded negatively in social science research. But it's not attended to. It's invisible. It's a happy, but unpursued by-product.

Alice: Well I like the idea of grounded practical theory but I'm not sure it's as novel as it's framing itself to be. In the recent *Communication Yearbook*, Shotter and Gergen had an essay on social constructionism that Barnett Pearce commented on.[3] Pearce said that taking a first-person perspective on issues or problems was a distinctive feature of communication as an academic discipline. I think that's true, although of course lots of people don't take that perspective. What he also said, which is really my point, is that this first-person problem perspective has been seen as less intellectual, not objective, or sophisticated. There's something of an irony there. Just as many communication researchers have gotten "intellectually respectable" by shucking off the first-person problem perspective, that perspective is gaining intellectual ascendance. So while I like the grounded practical theory notion, I'm not sure how different it is from what lots of others are writing now.

Rachel: You know, I just read Talbot Taylor's book on mutual misunderstandings.[4] He looks at five or six different theories of language and interpretation, showing how the core idea for each theory arises from taking some piece of the taken-for-granted practical world as problematic while accepting some other piece. Taylor seems to be arguing for the importance of practice too, but it's very different from the Craig notion that *Colloquium* builds on. Taylor doesn't seem to go past destabilizing and deconstructing theories, suggesting that everyday commonplaces inform them. Grounded practical theory critiques. But it also seeks to build. It blurs the line between understanding a practice, and cultivating it. It recognizes a researcher's connections with the people and practices he or she is studying. It's not prescriptive in the way that linguists rail against, but neither is it scientific and detached. Inquiry is purposeful and arises because there are communicative situations with real difficulties that are important to understand and improve.

[3.] See Shotter and Gergen (1994) and Pearce (1994).

[4.] See Talbot Taylor (1992).

Tom: I think John Dewey would happily claim practical theory as an offspring. It's a very pragmatic, Deweyan approach to inquiry. It seeks to keep theory, whatever that may be, and practice in a productive tension. You know, in discussing what makes for a good ethnography, Geertz talks about the importance of balancing experience-near and experience-distant perspectives.[5] Experience-near writing captures situations in their emotionally vivid and usually messy particulars; experience-distant identifies more general, universal issues. Both are essential and too much of one is disaster. As a field, I think our disasters have involved giving too much attention to the experience-distant perspective. Grounded practical theory would seem to offer a way to right the balance. It could be accused of going overboard but from my perspective it's much needed.

Ron: Let me shift gears a bit. We've been talking about approaches to inquiry at the metalevel. I'd like to move down a level of abstraction and say a few things about the kind of discourse analysis that *Colloquium* used. It seems to me that action-implicative discourse analysis offers a new option to those of us interested in language and social interaction. In your words, Tom, it's a recognizable offspring of, well three or four parents. But no one would confuse it with its intellectual parents. As I see it, action-implicative DA goes after a level of conversational inference that is particularly interesting—it's what we care about as people, how we're seen, the kinds of relationships we're making, how we create the climate or spirit of the groups we work in. It's a looser kind of analysis than you see in conversation analysis, but the looseness is worth it.

Alice: What do you mean by looser?

Ron: Well, conversation analysis as least as seen in the work of say Schegloff, Heritage or Drew focuses on describing the interactional meaning of particular conversational devices or procedures.[6] For instance, at a recent conference I attended, John Heritage discussed the use of "oh prefaces" in yes and

---

5. The concepts *experience-near* and *experience-distant* were developed by the psychoanalyst, Heinz Kohut. Geertz (1984) appropriates the terms to make a point about ethnography. "Confinement to experience-near concepts leaves an ethnographer awash in immediacies, as well as entangled in vernacular. Confinement to experience-distant ones leaves him stranded in abstractions and smothered in jargon" (p. 124).

6. See Atkinson and Drew (1979), Atkinson and Heritage (1984), and Schegloff (1979, 1989).

no answers.[7] That is, what's the difference between saying "yes" and "oh yes" and "no" and "oh no"? Heritage's presentation systematically proceeded through ten or fifteen instances of these "oh" prefaces. At the end he had made a pretty strong case about the function of these things. I found the presentation fascinating. And I was persuaded. But I can't imagine doing that kind of work myself. It doesn't get back fast enough to the rhetorical level of communicators making choices, issues of better and worse courses of action. Action-implicative discourse analysis, at least as displayed by Tracy, doesn't have that airtight quality to its analytic interpretations that good CA work does. But on the other hand, it covers more ground. I think the name captures its major strength: It is more implicative for communicative action.

Todd: That's kind of funny. From my vantage point as a rhetorician, I thought *Colloquium* got too detailed. I felt as if the importance of intellectual discussion as a communicative activity got lost. In focusing on the details so much, it trivialized the substance of discussions. It devalued what it wrote about by not taking the issues people argued about seriously. In addition, all those uhms and ahs made people sound like dolts.

Ron: How can you say that? That's the way people really talk. Including us, Todd. But speaking to your major point, I would draw just the opposite conclusion. *Colloquium* affirms the importance of this kind of talking by looking at it so carefully. Thinking of intellectual discussion as a neutral conduit in which ideas engage with each other is ridiculous. I think the book made that point pretty clearly.

Todd: I'd agree with your last statement about discussion not being a neutral conduit but not that that level of detail is needed.

[*pause*]

Elise: Let me change the focus a bit. One of the things that intrigued me about action-implicative discourse analysis was the particular way it combined analysis of interview and interactive discourse. Treating interviews as discourse is not a new thing. Lots of discourse analysts have done that. Mishler, van Dijk, Edwards and Potter.[8] Nor is looking in

---

7. See Heritage (1995).

8. See van Dijk (1987), Mishler (1986), and Edwards and Potter (1992).

detail at the discourse in an institutional setting. What I
think is new is the conceptual link between the two.
Colloquium suggests how to explore the character of problems and situated ideals in interviews, and link these to conversational strategies. Conceiving of the interviews as
metadiscourse about colloquium discourse seems useful. I
don't know if any of you saw it, but in a recent issue of
Research on Language and Social Interaction there was short
colloquy between the editors, Sanders and Sigman, and
Tracy.[9] Sanders and Sigman questioned whether interviews
should be considered as language and social interaction
research and Tracy argued for the value of doing so. I don't
think Tracy has worked out all the problems involved in
linking interview and interactive discourse but *Colloquium*
offers a good start.

[*pause*]

Alice: How about we turn our attention to the second discussion
question?

IMPLICATIONS FOR FUTURE THEORY AND RESEARCH?

Alice: In the last year or two I've been getting into the rhetoric of
inquiry, the sociology of knowledge, people like Gilbert and
Mulkay, Knorr-Cetina, Latour and Woolgar.[10] One of the
things I found myself thinking about as I was reading
Colloquium was the idea of situational frame. Tracy uses intellectual discussion to understand what the discussants at her
colloquia are doing. But, what difference would it make if the
colloquium had been framed as "talking science" or something like that. It's true that most studies within the sociology
of knowledge have focused on chemistry, biology or whatever.
But, not all of them have. McKinlay and Potter published a
piece in *Social Studies of Science* where they examined the talk

---

9. See Sanders and Sigman (1994) and Tracy (1994).

10. See Knorr-Cetina (1981), and Latour and Woolgar (1986), Lynch (1985) for interpretations of how scientific knowledge is constructed through everyday laboratory practices.
Gilbert and Mulkay (1984) provide a particularly intriguing analysis of the differences in how
scientists talk about their own work and that of scientific competitors, and Bunge (1991,
1992) reviews this entire line of research.

of social psychologists at a conference.[11] Interestingly, they titled the paper something like "Interpretative Repertories in Scientists' Talk." What struck me was that the news of their paper rested on framing the psychologists' talk as "science." By that I mean that the article's interest value arose from showing that "scientists" talked in ways that were not necessarily objective, truth-seeking, and factual. They showed that psychologists' talk was rhetorical, designed to accomplish interpersonal aims which varied from one moment in time to the next. Consider what difference it makes if we describe the social psychologists' talk as intellectual discussion rather than science talk. Basically, the intellectual discussion frame makes the finding that participants are strategic and arguing about things that others could see differently, uninteresting. Who would think otherwise? Intellectual discussion implies that people are talking about matters of truth that can never be known with absolute certainty.

Reid: I'm not sure if I've understood where you're going but let me free associate. Allen Grimshaw has edited a book where lots of people write about twelve minutes from a dissertation defense.[12] In the opening to the book, he offers three different frames for the event. One frame he gives to the defense is "professional conversation." Another is "cross-status conflict," and still another is "ritual." Each of these three frames is different. Each draws our attention to certain features of the interaction and away from others. For instance, if Tracy had used professional conversation or cross-status conflict as the main frame for colloquium, then it seems unlikely the tensions surrounding equality/expertise would either have been noticed or regarded as interesting. In a situation that is fundamentally defined as participants of unequal statuses, it is not newsworthy to notice that everyone is not treated equally. So if a situational frame shapes whether something will be noticed or regarded as interesting, what does that

---

[11.] McKinlay and Potter (1987). See also Potter (1984). Another example of increasing the newsworthiness of an author's claim is seen in Greg Myers's (1989) analysis of the politeness devices in scientific writing. While most of his work has focused on biologists (1990), in the politeness article he uses linguists Brown and Levinson as his scientists.

[12.] Grimshaw (1994) edited a volume in which a set of linguists, anthropologists, and sociologists comment on different facets of a sociology dissertation defense. Grimshaw (1989) writes about this same dissertation defense in considerably more detail in his earlier book.

mean about how scholars should select situational frames? Is frame selection constrained in any way?

Alice: Thanks Reid, that reminds me of what I was trying to say. What I was trying to get at is this. When we academics write and talk about communicative situations, we often do so as if the frame we have selected were the only one that could fit. We treat the selected frame as transparently obvious, not requiring any justification. Too, the news of what we report often rests on our frame in ways of which we're not fully aware. My point is not that there is always more than one frame, and frame selection influences what will be noticed or interesting—that's true—but I want to go past that. What I'm trying to say is that there is no single right way to frame an occasion. What actually occurs in the talk will make some small set of frames salient. But each different frame will influence what is noticed to be in the talk. I think intellectual discussion is a reasonable frame for academic discussion but it's clearly not the only one.

Reid: This discussion of frames ties to a point I wanted to make about text and context and how *Colloquium* solves a problem I've been thinking about with regard to Brown and Levinson's politeness theory.[13] Brown and Levinson, as many of you know, develop a theory that seeks to explain why people talk as they do in a whole bunch of different situations. Their theory treats situations as differing in three ways: how close or distant people are, whether people are equal or one is higher status, and how big an imposition different kinds of communicative acts involve. So, in politeness theory it is assumed that every act, depending on its amount of imposition and the kind of relationship in which it's occurring, involves face-threat to one or another party. For instance, criticizing another is primarily threatening that person's positive face—his or her desire to be seen as competent and likeable. In Brown and Levinson's theory, people calculate the amount of face-threat implied by an act and then select the appropriate conversational strategy. If an act is highly face-threatening, a person is likely to select the least threatening strategy. And in their system that means that, shall we say speaker Sam, is likely to avoid the face-threatening act altogether. The problem with this logic is that it fails to account for something we all know is true. That offense can be caused by not doing something.

[13.] Brown and Levinson (1987).

Colloquium showed that in this intellectual discussion context where criticizing and disagreeing are expected activities, to not criticize can be the most threatening act of all.

Tim: So is your point just that one cannot not communicate?

Reid: No, no it's more particular than that. I think it is possible to "not communicate." At the colloquium if I fail to comment about the weather or mention where my sister is traveling, you're unlikely to notice it. You won't attach any meaning to the absence of those actions. They are not expected. But criticizing is expected in this intellectual discussion context. So its absence is significant. Just like the dog that didn't bark in the night was a cue for Sherlock Holmes. Every context creates expectations. This means that any attempt to categorize acts as face-threatening without attention to the particulars of the situation is doomed. That's Brown and Levinson's problem.

Tim: Let me ask a question and see what the rest of you think. It seemed to me that the notion of dilemma slipped around and changed throughout the book. On the one hand it referred to an ideological level, contrary values or belief differences like the equality/ expertise dilemma. On the other, it was used in a more behavioral sense to refer to specific action choices such as reading or speaking extemporaneously, asking a tough question or an easy one, and so on. This inconsistency bothered me and I wondered what the rest of you thought.

Ellen: I think you're right. Dilemma did take on different meanings at different points in the book. But I didn't see that, if you will, "inconsistency" as a problem. In fact, it led me to an insight. In the *Ideological Dilemmas* book,[14] Billig and his coauthors make a big deal of distinguishing the traditional focus of social psychology on choice dilemmas—Do I take a job at Harvard where I have 10% chance of getting tenured or Podunk U where I have a 60% chance?—versus dilemmas that arise from inconsistencies in holding two contrary values. But there's another kind of dilemma. I'd call it an interactional dilemma. An interactional dilemma concerns how a person should talk and act at a particular moment. Then we have Billig's ideological dilemmas that are about values and beliefs. But rather than distinct types of dilemmas, I think it's more useful to think of them as conceptual anchors on a continuum. Some dilemmas are more at the level of interaction, others at the ideological

---

14. Billig et al. (1988).

level, and still others are better thought of as a hybrid. But whatever is the salient face of the dilemma, I think the other face is always implicated. That is, values and beliefs have to be translated into conversational actions, and interactional choices are consequential because of what they mean in terms of values and more deep-seated beliefs.

If you buy the claim that the ideological and interactional are two facets of every dilemma, then there is a second issue. How do the two get linked? About a decade ago Eric Eisenberg wrote an article on the use of strategic ambiguity in organizations and I think his idea is relevant here.[15] That is, I see the link between ideology and interaction as inherently ambiguous. And that is not a bad thing but an asset, a resource. It's the ambiguity of the link that makes possible communicative creativity, managing problems in satisfactory ways. For instance, if we focus on the colloquium setting, it may be the case that critiquing an idea on its merit and critiquing it in a way that takes account of the expertise of the other is an ideological dilemma. But the actual kinds of choices people have in terms of talking—what words they say, how fast, with what kind of facial expression and intonation—is a very different level of choice. More telling, it's not that easy to relate conversational choices to the ideological level. Is using a mitigated form to disagree, a device to recognize one's essential equality with another or is it evidence that the speaker is higher status and is trying to be gentle and thoughtful in dealings with the other? Or some nastier interpretation? Similarly, while two conversational actions may be absolutely incompatible—a person can only do one or the other—what the action signifies may not be. Different actions against a certain contextual backdrop, and with a bit of rhetorical work, can count as evidence of the same value. This is not to argue that anything goes—it doesn't—but it is recognizing the artful component of any meaning that gets accepted.

[*pause*]

IMPLICATIONS FOR ACADEMIC CONDUCT?

Rachel: Not to change the topic but what do you think about the proposals for cultivating practice? It's not clear to me that

---

15. Eisenberg (1984).

reading this book will make us, or let me speak for myself—me—a better discussant.

Reid: Yeah, I know what you mean. But I'm not sure what a fair standard is. That is, in what ways do ideas—the stuff we read in books—ever affect action? Think about our faculty meetings. Here we are, a group of people who collectively possess a vast amount of expertise about group problem-solving and decision-making. Would you know that by looking at our faculty meetings? I doubt it. Now maybe that says more about our theories of group processes than it does about us as people. But regardless, it suggests that linking ideas about action, to action is fraught with difficulty. I found *Colloquium* thought-provoking but I'd be hard pressed to say how I'm going to act differently.

Ellen: Well it got me thinking about some of the ways I felt when I was a graduate student. I remember feeling like my major professors were always putting me in a double bind. They'd explicitly encourage me to be assertive, stand up for my views, argue my point, but then I'd do that on some occasion and I'd get a pretty strong message to shut up and do as I was told, recognize their superior expertise. The insight I had reading the book is that I had failed to see I was doing the same thing to them. Well not exactly the same thing, they had the power. But, I was instructing them, if you will, to take me seriously, and treat me as an equal, while also expecting them to recognize my lesser experience and "be fair"—not expect too much of me. It's been awhile since graduate school so I've become more familiar with the problems from a faculty member's point of view and I've been aware of the double bind students put me in. But I hadn't related it back to myself as a student. That is, ((laugh)) I guess it's easier to identify how the other person is acting unreasonably. It's in that sense that I think reading *Colloquium* may improve how I act, or at least think. I think I'll be a little less quick to judge my colleagues and students as jerks, pretentious asses, morons, whatever.

Joseph: Speaking as a graduate student, I had several rather different reactions. Part of me delighted in seeing faculty actions, if you will, exposed. There's a certain satisfaction in seeing the motives of your, your intellectual betters revealed to be less than pure. But I would basically agree with Ellen. Reading *Colloquium* has made me more sympathetic to the difficulties faculty must encounter dealing with us. It also legitimated my experience as a graduate student. To use some of the loaded language the book referred to, it made me see that the "ego" concerns I have are not all bad; they serve a positive function. And, it's good to know that lots of people worry about saying stupid things and being seen as ignorant. It's nice to know you're normal!

Rachel: Actually, the excerpts from the discussions gave me ideas about things I could say in this situation that I'd never thought about before. I feel as if I have a few more strategies at my disposal for the next time I present.

Tim: I don't know. Reading the book made me completely self-conscious. I felt foolish at last week's colloquium when I presented my paper because I could hear all of the things that I was saying—this paper grew out of blah, blah, blah—that I wouldn't have been aware of before. I didn't like that. And I don't think it made my presentation better.

Ron: I can see your point. I'll probably feel the same way at my next presentation but don't you think that kind of self-consciousness passes quickly and is a necessary part of becoming more reflective about yourself and how to accomplish what you want?

Tim: Maybe. But maybe not. I'll let you know how I feel in a couple of weeks.

Reid: Let me broaden the scope of our discussion a bit. An issue I was thinking about as I was reading the book is our academic notions of thought and thinking, and what we're doing here in universities. We have a course in critical thinking, as do other departments, as well as lots of other schools. College students are expected to learn how to think critically. And, the courses we teach, but particularly the critical thinking course, are presumed to help students do this better. Now what do we do in the critical thinking course? Basically, we try to teach students to better analyze writing and talking. Does an argument hold together? Is the evidence sufficient for the claim? Are there any reasoning fallacies? And so on. Now don't get me wrong. I think this is important to do and we generally do a decent job. But, are we really cultivating students' abilities to think critically? Will they go past the texts we analyze in classes and apply this in their daily lives? When they leave our classes, will they think in ways that generate more thoughtful, defensible responses to the personal, work and societal problems they encounter? I'm not so sure. In certain ways, even, we may even be doing something harmful in the classroom. Implicitly, critical thinking instruction reinforces a view of thinking as a detached, disembodied, completely cognitive, asocial thing. Now lots of people are arguing against this view; I think particularly of Mark Johnson and George Lakoff.[16] But nonetheless those notions haven't seeped into the classroom.[17] *Colloquium* makes a case for the importance of the social. It suggests that building a sense of trust and caring among students is essential if you want to get them willing to risk saying dumb things that can become grist for critical thinking.

Ed: Can I interrupt? I just wrote a paper on Lakoff's *Women, Fire and Dangerous Things* and I have it here. I want to read a quote that I really like that I think is relevant. Lakoff says, "How we understand the mind matters . . . for what we value in ourselves and others—for education, for research, for the ways we set up human institutions, and most important for what counts as a humane way to live and act."[18] Isn't that nice?

Reid: I like what Lakoff has to say about reasoning being rooted in our bodily and imaginative experiences, but he doesn't give much attention to the social dimension of thinking. That it's an activity that occurs in people's lives; it's something we do with each other. Ochs and some of her students recently published a paper where they analyze a family dinner table conversation.[19] They argue that it is the kind of storytelling that people do in families that fosters the seeds of scientific reasoning. It is in this context that kids are learning to be open-minded, defend their points of view, and challenge others. I think that's the same point *Colloquium* is making in the section on community. Trusting relationships are preconditions for certain kinds of talk. And, that means certain kinds of thinking.

[16.] See Johnson (1987) and Lakoff (1987).

[17.] Actually, the speaker is overstating his case. Arnett (1992) argues for "dialogic education" as a model for classes. Dialogic education seeks to recognize that education is "conversation about ideas between people."

[18.] See Lakoff (1987, p. xvi).

[19.] See Ochs, Taylor, Rudolph, and Smith (1992).

Ellen: But what does that mean for big state universities like ours? It's not going to happen in the typical college classroom. Maybe at small private colleges where students have contact with the same group of students over time, and where socializing between faculty and students happens. But setting up experiences in large universities like ours would be difficult. And it would certainly take money.

Rhonda: I'm not sure if this is connected, but I wanted to make a comment about an analogy that came up in one of the interviews. I think it was in the cultivation chapter. Somebody said how intellectual discussion was a dance of ideas and personalities. I liked that analogy and it got me thinking. Surprised, aren't you?

[*group laughter*]

Ed: Who's got a gag? We're going to get another dance lecture!

Rhonda: Yep, you are! Well, I was thinking of what's involved in two people learning how to dance well together. If you're going to get into any fun, interesting dancing, you have to go through a phase of stepped-on toes. The only way to entirely avoid stepped-on toes, is to do the conventional. Now the more practiced you get with a particular partner, the more novel and intricate maneuvers you can pull off, unpracticed if you will. Good dancing requires more than two good dancers—it requires experience with the other. Returning to intellectual discussion, getting to good discussion requires putting up with some toe-stepping. If avoiding stepping on toes, guides what you attempt, you'll never get that kind of discussion that is the real intellectual high—where everyone is so involved in the talk that self is forgotten.

Rachel: We're running out of time, but let me take advantage of my role as discussion organizer to say one last thing. If I were to say what I took away from this book at a practical level, it would be the value of posing a set of questions when I confront a difficulty: What's the other part of the problem I'm facing? What's the hidden feature? What else do I take to be important in this situation that I'm not recognizing right off the bat? I don't think all communicative problems are dilemmatic. But lots of them are. I think this frame helps me make sense of our colloquium, and I think it's helpful for other occasions.

[*pause*]

Rachel: THE END. See you all next week for David's presentation about staff conflicts in a neighborhood mediation center.

Appendix A

State U Interviews

OVERVIEW

Interviews at State U were conducted with 10 regular participants. Six of the participants were faculty; of those six, one was female. Four of the interviewees were graduate students with one being male. At State U, roughly two-thirds of the graduate students were female and one-third male. At any point in time there were usually a few African-American, Asian-American, or non-U.S. students; the vast majority of students, however, were Americans of European background. Interviews were conducted by a graduate student in the program. That the interviewer was a graduate student is reflected in the ways interviewees formulated answers to specific questions.

All interviews were audiotaped and transcribed. Below is the interview schedule that was used as a rough guide. Exact question wording varied as a goal of the interview was to create rapport with the interviewee. The interviewer worked to capture the gist of questions in the interview schedule while making exact question formulations responsive to what an interviewee had just previously said. Questions were also probed when interviewees made comments that seemed worth exploring.

INTERVIEW SCHEDULE

I. Goals of the Colloquium

1. What do you see as the purpose of the colloquium? What do you feel is its role in the graduate program?

2. If you were to ask the faculty (graduate students) what the purpose of the colloquium is, what do you think they would say?

3. Does colloquium have other purposes than the officially stated ones? Can you think of any occasion that gives evidence of that?

II. Presenting Role

4. What do you think are the typical concerns of presenters? If you were to present, what would (or were) your main concerns be?

5. Do you think faculty and graduate students have similar concerns about giving a presentation? How? Why?

III. Discussion Period

6. Every week there are different topics followed by a discussion. To what degree do you think the issues that come up in the colloquia are the same across weeks? If so, what are they?

7. What 2 to 3 people do you see as the most active participants? Why?

8. If you had to identify the 1 to 2 people whose comments you found most consistently interesting, who would they be?

9. What do you see as the role of the faculty (graduate students) in colloquium? What might their concerns be regarding their role? (individually or collectively)

10. Describe your role in colloquium.

11. Do you have any concerns about your role in colloquium?

12. How do you think faculty (grad students) see you in colloquium? Other graduate students (faculty)?

13. Would you say people get a fairly good sample of your "intellectual self" at colloquium? Why or why not?

14. Would you say you get a fairly good sample of the "intellectual self" of others at colloquium? Why or why not?

15. Do you have any concerns in formulating the questions you ask or comments you make during the discussion period? Do you ever edit your comments?

IV. Miscellaneous

16 Explain colloquium to a friend outside department.

17. What do you think of the "five minute rule"?

18. In what ways could colloquium be improved?
19. What faculty members do your interests align with most closely?
20. Anything you want to add?

Appendix B

University X Interviews

OVERVIEW

Interviewees included 13 faculty, seven junior faculty, and six senior faculty. Among the junior faculty were five assistant professors and two instructors. Of the junior faculty all were female except one. Among the senior faculty all were male; two of the participants were associate professors, the rest were full professors. Of the seven graduate student attenders, four were first-year students. Three students were female; four were male. One participant was African American; all others were Americans of European background.

Individual interviews were conducted with participants over several months. Approximately half of the interviews were conducted by me; the other half by a graduate student in the program. All interviews with graduate students, except the interview of the graduate student interviewer, were conducted by the graduate student. I assumed that graduate students would feel more free about speaking in front of another graduate student than a faculty member. The interview with the graduate student interviewer that I conducted as the first interview was included.

Interviews were conducted in locations convenient for the interviewee—in the person's office, his or her home, a quiet restaurant, or outside on a campus bench. Interviews averaged about an hour in length, varying from 30 to 80 minutes; graduate student interviews tended to be the shorter. All interviews were audiotaped and transcribed.

The central question that guided development of the interview schedule was to understand what academics believed to be good discussion and how it was typically achieved. I assumed that the best way to understand this was to have people reflect about the discussions in which they routinely participated as well as to discuss their beliefs about what intellectual discussion generally should look like.

INTERVIEW SCHEDULE

I. Departmental Colloquium

1. What three things do you like most and what three things do you like least about the colloquium?
2. Do you have any concerns about how you present yourself in colloquium? What are they?
3. In what ways do you think faculty (student) concerns are similar to your own? Differ from your own?
4. Have you gotten a sense of other people's "intellectual selves" through their participation? How so?
5. Do you think people have gotten a sense of your "intellectual self"? Why or why not?
6. Have you had other experiences similar to this colloquium? Tell me about them. In what ways were they similar to the colloquium? Different?
7. How often did you attend the colloquium? Why? When you attended, how would you describe your participation?

II. Intellectual Discussion

8. If I say the phrase *intellectual discussion*, what comes to mind? What is an intellectual discussion?
9. If you think about different kinds of talk, intellectual discussion being one kind, what are the other kinds of talk people do with each other?
10. In what other settings besides the university do intellectual discussions occur?
11. How well does the colloquium fit your definition of intellectual discussion?
12. Are most classroom discussions intellectual discussion? Why or why not?
13. What are the purposes of intellectual discussion?

14. If you had to identify the features that would distinguish a good intellectual discussion from a bad one, what would they be?

15. What role do you think criticism should have in intellectual discussion?

16. What role do you think praise should have in intellectual discussion?

17. What kind of climate best promotes intellectual discussion? Explain.

18. To what degree do you think people express their feelings during intellectual discussion? In what ways does expression of feelings contribute to a good discussion? In what ways does it hinder good discussion?

19. Is equality among participants necessary for a good discussion? Why or why not?

20. In what ways, if any, do you think the discussion following someone's presentation of his or her work differs from the discussion where a group reads a common reading?

21. How important is the ability to present and orally defend one's ideas for academic success? Why do you think so?

22. How would you compare the relative importance of writing and speaking abilities for academic success? Why?

23. What are the kinds of things a person would say or do during an intellectual discussion like the colloquium that would lead you to be impressed with the person?

24. What are the kinds of things a person would say or do that would lead you to be unimpressed with a person?

25. What inferences, if any, might you draw about a person if he or she was routinely silent during discussion? What about if a person were silent on a specific occasion?

26. Are there any comments you'd like to make about intellectual discussion or colloquium that I haven't asked about?

Appendix C

Supplemental Discussion Materials

In addition to the colloquium discussions at State U, examples are taken from three other kinds of intellectual discussions.

COMMUNICATION ASSOCIATION SEMINAR

In 1986 an all-day seminar occurred at a national communication conference. The seminar was organized by several scholars in communication who had interests in ethnography of speaking. The session was taped and made available for purchase through the national association. I did not participate in this session but received the tapes through a colleague.

The seminar included seven paper presenters and several other observer-participants. Participants could be characterized as sharing a research tradition that was respected but was a nondominant one in the communication field. At the day's start, the seminar organizer overviewed the procedure suggesting that each presenter would have 30 minutes, 15 minutes to give the paper and 15 minutes for discussion. Participants roughly followed this schedule, though some spoke more than 15 minutes, and more than 30 minutes was spent on certain papers.

The discussion periods from the day's session of seven papers were transcribed. Several examples from these discussions are used.

ANNA SMITH'S DISSERTATION DEFENSE

One instance in the book is taken from a dissertation defense at State U. The dissertation defense involved a Ph.D. student, four faculty members from the State U communication department, of which I was one, and a faculty member from the business school. No other parties attended the defense. The student had taped the defense to assist herself in doing any revisions that the committee would request. She gave me a copy of the tape following completion of her degree.

The format of this dissertation defense had strong similarities with the weekly colloquium. The defense began with a short presentation by the student in which she summarized the study she had done and the main claims she was making. Then faculty members questioned her about the research. Questioning was more evenly distributed than at the typical colloquium in that each faculty member was given a turn, designated at the start by the student's advisor, to question the student. Like colloquia in which a person's presentation was part of a job interview, an explicitly evaluative metaframe surrounded the intellectual presentation/discussion involved in this dissertation defense: How intellectually compelling were the ideas and arguments? How much rewriting did the student need to do? In that sense, while the discussion itself was not a vehicle for making a decision, the student's ability to participate in and manage the discussion became a criterion that affected the decision outcome.

As Grimshaw (1989) has noted, it is rare for dissertation defenses to result in a "fail" judgment. Most dissertation defenses do not occur until the involved faculty judge the student's work to merit a "pass" judgment. However while "fail" is an unlikely outcome, the committee does make a decision about the extensiveness of the rewriting required of the student and about how many people are to be involved in supervising the rewriting. This decision is partly influenced by the student's intellectual performance in the presentation/discussion.

STATE U FACULTY SYMPOSIUM

During the academic year 1983–1984, the College of Arts and Sciences at State U sponsored a faculty symposium. The symposium was part of the Distinguished Professor program introduced for the first time in that year. The recipient of the Distinguished Professor Award—a philosophy professor—gave a series of public lectures over the year and led a faculty seminar on the "Human Sciences and the Unity of Science."

In April of the prior year, the dean of the college sent a memo to faculty, inviting faculty to apply to be considered as participants in the seminar for the following year, a seminar to be restricted to 20 participants. Selected faculty included individuals of all institutional ranks from 11 different departments. In addition to the official participants, all in the university were invited to attend the discussion. In addition, a second tier of membership involvement was created by a written memo that identified the 25 additional faculty who were interested in doing the readings and attending to observe. I was in the second tier of faculty. The seminar met in a large circular room that could accommodate several hundred. The official participants sat in the inner circle and others sat around the room. The seminar went for two and a half hours with a break for refreshments in the middle. Attendance at the seminar decreased markedly across the year's time. My sense is that there were around 75 to 100 people present for the first several occasions but that this was down to 20 to 30 by the year's end.

In a preseminar memo the purpose of the seminar was described as:

> to examine selected texts from a group of particularly influential theorists ranging over the so-called human sciences with attention to the prospects of a new unified view of the sciences. The approach will be interdisciplinary and will draw materials from both the Anglo-American and Continental traditions. Possible authors include: Claude Lévi-Strauss, Thomas Kuhn, Louis Althusser, Michel Foucault, Jurgen Habermas, Noam Chomsky, Jean Piaget, Hans-Georg Gadamer, Jacques Derrida.

The entire seminar was taped by media staff at the university and the tapes were made available to interested parties. A transcription of the second session focusing on Adorno and the early Frankfurt School was made. This symposium, and the Adorno session in particular, served as an implicit comparison point for the chapter on intellectual community. In essence, I asked, "What goes on in State U's colloquium that we do not see in a group in which participants are relative strangers in a high-visibility discussion?" One of the most notable features was the comparative frequency of very long comments. Discussants' comments had a preplanned flavor. Not only were comments long and loosely connected to a prior comment, but it was not unusual to see discussants referring to written notes to offer a comment.

This symposium and State U's colloquium differed in a number of ways besides the relational difference noted above. The group's audience was larger, and the symposium's discussion task was different. The group discussed a set of articles rather than responding to a single presenter. Because of these multiple differences (and because of the extensive background knowledge required to understand the group's discussion), I do not quote excerpts from the discussion. Instead, the symposium is used as a point of comparison to inform the analysis of State U's colloquium.

Appendix D

Transcription

As many discourse analysts (e.g., Coupland, 1988; Craig & Tracy, 1983; Ochs, 1979) have noted, transcribing is an activity that involves choices about what to record (or ignore) and how to note particulars. Over the past 15 years, a number of distinctive transcription systems have developed. Schiffrin's (1994) introduction to discourse analysis provides an overview of several of the more visible systems. Included in her introduction is a comparison of the Jeffersonian system (Atkinson & Heritage, 1984), a system developed by conversation analysts that is perhaps the most widely used one, and several others developed and adopted by linguists (e.g., Schiffrin, 1987; Tannen, 1989). In each of these systems, different aspects of pronunciation, vocal rhythm and stress, and timing are captured.

In contrast to the transcription systems referred to above, I have chosen a relatively simple one that extends the conventions of standard orthography. Transcripts capture words, restarts (dec-, decimate), and repairs (I want, I want, could I ask), and vocalized nonfluencies (uh or uhm), but generally do not attend to vocalic or timing information. Three reasons warranted transcribing at this broad level. First, and most importantly, action-implicative discourse analysis is primarily interested in identifying conversational strategies about which people are capable of reflecting as they contemplate action. While there is no question that prosodic and timing features of conversation influence particular situated meanings, these features are less likely to be within the conscious control of communicators, and hence are less promising avenues for a discourse analyst interested in cultivating practice. Second, at a very practical level there is a trade-off between the amount of conversation one can examine and the detail with which it is transcribed. Given the nature of this project, a greater breadth of materials at a more limited transcription depth seemed a wiser choice than detailed transcription of a more limited number of instances. Finally, the project was intended for an interdisciplinary audience so it was important to minimize the use of a technical notation system and make transcripts accessible for readers of diverse backgrounds.

TRANSCRIPTION CONVENTIONS

CAPS   This indicates speech that is louder and more emphatic.

!   This indicates that speaker is exclaiming.

-    Hyphen indicates syllable that is abruptly cut off

" "   in excerpts; quotation marks indicate reported speech

( )   Parentheses indicate transcriptionist doubt. Length of parentheses offers rough indicator of length of undecipherable speech

(( ))   Double parentheses are used to describe interactional style or nonspeech activity. For example ((group laughter)) or ((pause))

{ }   Braces are used to indicate that a specific word has been replaced with a category term. For instance, if a speaker said "in the speech accommodation literature, it's been documented that," the transcript might read "in the {name of literature} it's been documented that."

[ ]   Brackets are used to cue explanatory material added by the analyst.

. . .   Three-dot ellipsis is used to indicate that a segment of text has been elided.

italics   Italics are used to draw attention to a particular segment that is the focus of an analytic point

NOTES

1. With the exception of specifics noted above, punctuation and capitalization have been added to aid readability. While in many cases the use of these conventions co-occurs with certain intonation patterns—periods going with the falling intonation used at the end of sentences and commas going with a continuing intonation—transcripts were not checked for intonational correspondence.

2. All name references to people in the situation were changed. In changing names in the transcripts, gender and form of name (first, last) were retained. While the names of participants talking, and the students and colleagues they refer to have been changed, names of authors that are part of a comment about an issue being discussed are usually retained. For instance, in Excerpt 58, the speaker said "*Parallel Lives* by Phyllis Rose," and that is included in the body of the excerpt. However, when it was thought that an involved party might experience embarrassment from a potentially unflattering analytic point, and the content made the speaker's identity too easily guessable for departmental members, I have changed the reference to a category one and have indicated this in the text with braces.

References

Adler, P. A., & Adler, P. (1987). *Membership roles in field research*. Newbury Park, CA: Sage.

Albrecht, T. L., & Hall, B. J. (1991). Facilitating talk about new ideas: The role of personal relationships in organizational innovation. *Communication Monographs, 58*, 272–288.

Anderson, J. A. (1987). *Communication research: Issues and methods*. New York: McGraw–Hill.

Anderson, W. T. (1986). The apostolic function of the dentist. In S. Fisher & A. D. Todd (Eds.), *Discourse and institutional authority: Medicine, education and law* (pp. 78–90). Norwood, NJ: Ablex.

Antaki, C. (1994). *Explaining and arguing: The social organization of accounts*. London: Sage.

Aristotle. (1941). *Ethica Nicomachea* (W. D. Ross, Trans.) In R. McKeon (Ed.), *The basic works of Aristotle* (pp. 927–1112). NY: Random House.

Arnett, R. C. (1992). *Dialogic education: Conversation about ideas and between people*. Carbondale: Southern Illinois Press.

Aronsson, K. (1991). Social interaction and the recycling of legal evidence. In N. Coupland, H. Giles, & J. M. Wiemann (Eds.), *"Miscommunication" and problematic talk* (pp. 215–243). Newbury Park, CA: Sage.

Aronsson, K., & Rundstrom, B. (1989). Cats, dogs, and sweets in the clinical negotiation of reality: On politeness and coherence in pediatric discourse. *Language in Society, 18*, 483–504.

Atkinson, J. M., & Drew, P. (1979). *Order in court: The organisation of verbal interaction in judicial settings*. London: Macmillan.

Atkinson, J. M., & Heritage, J. (Eds.). (1984). *Structure of social action: Studies in conversation analysis*. Cambridge, England: Cambridge University Press.

Bailey, F. G. (1983). *The tactical uses of passion*. Ithaca, NY: Cornell University Press.

Basso, K. (1979). *Portraits of "The Whiteman": Linguistic play and cultural symbols among the Western Apache*. New York: Cambridge University Press.

Bateson, G. (1972). *Steps to an ecology of mind*. New York: Ballantine.

Baumeister, R. F. (Ed.). (1986). *Public and private self*. New York: Springer–Verlag.

Baxter, L.A. (1988). A dialectical perspective on communication strategies in relationship development. In S. Duck, D. Hay, S. Hobfoll, W. Ickes, & B. Montgomery (Eds.), *Handbook of personal relationships: Theory, research and interventions* (pp. 257–274). Chichester, England: Wiley.

Baxter, L.A., & Montgomery, B.M. (1996), *Relating: Dialogues and dialectics.* New York: Guilford.

Bazerman, C. (1988). *Shaping written knowledge: The genre and activity of the experimental article in science.* Madison: University of Wisconsin Press.

Bazerman, C., & Paradis, J. (1991). Introduction. In C. Bazerman & J. Paradis (Eds.), *Textual dynamics of the professions* (pp. 3–10). Madison: University of Wisconsin Press.

Becher, T. (1989). *Academic tribes and territories: Intellectual inquiry and the culture of disciplines.* Milton Keynes, England: Open University Press.

Belenky, M. F., Clinchy, B. M., Goldberger, N. R., & Tarule, J. M. (1986). *Women's ways of knowing.* New York: Basic Books.

Bellah, R. N., Madsen, W. M., Swidler, A., & Tipton, S. M. (1985). *Habits of the heart.* New York: Harper & Row.

Bellah, R. N., Madsen, W. M., Swidler, A., & Tipton, S. M. (1992). *The good society.* New York: Vintage.

Billig, M. (1986). *Thinking and arguing.* Inaugural lecture. Loughborough University, Loughborough, England.

Billig, M. (1987). *Arguing and thinking: A rhetorical approach to social psychology.* Cambridge, England: Cambridge University Press.

Billig, M., Condor, S., Edwards, D., Gane, M., Middleton, D., & Radley, A. (1988). *Ideological dilemmas.* London: Sage.

Bizzell, P. (1992). *Academic discourse and critical consciousness.* Pittsburgh: University of Pittsburgh Press.

Bowers, J. W., & Courtright, J. A. (1984). *Communication research methods.* Glenview, IL: Scott, Foresman.

Bowers, J. W., Metts, S. M., & Duncanson, W. T. (1985). Emotion and interpersonal communication. In M. L. Knapp & G. R. Miller (Eds.), *Handbook of interpersonal communication* (pp. 500–550). Beverly Hills, CA: Sage.

Boynton, G. R. (1991). When senators and publics meet at the environmental protection subcommittee. *Discourse and Society, 2,* 131–156.

Brown, P., & Levinson, S. C. (1987). *Universals in language usage: Politeness phenomena.* Cambridge, England: Cambridge University Press.

Brown, R., & Gilman, A. (1989). Politeness theory and Shakespeare's four major tragedies. *Language in Society, 18,* 159–212.

Browne, M. N., & Keeley, S. M. (1990). *Asking the right question: A guide to critical thinking* (3rd Ed.). Englewood Cliffs, NJ: Prentice–Hall.

Bunge, M. (1991). A critical examination of the new sociology of science, Part I. *Philosophy of the Social Sciences, 21,* 524–560.

Bunge, M. (1992). A critical examination of the new sociology of science, Part II. *Philosophy of the Social Sciences, 22,* 46–76.

Burke, K. (1966). *Language as symbolic action.* Berkeley, CA: University of California Press.

Buttny, R. (1990). Blame–account sequences in therapy: The negotiation of relational meanings. *Semiotica, 78,* 219–247.

Buttny, R., & Cohen, J. R. (1991). The uses of goals in therapy. In K. Tracy (Ed.), *Understanding face-to-face interaction: Issues linking goals and discourse* (pp. 63–77). Hillsdale, NJ: Erlbaum.

Cappella, J. N., & Street, Jr., R. L. (1985). Introduction: A functional approach to the structure of communicative behaviour. In R. L. Street & J. N. Cappella (Eds.), *Sequence and pattern in communicative behaviour* (pp. 1–29). London: Edward Arnold.

Carbaugh, D. (1988). *Talking American.* Norwood, NJ: Ablex.

Cicourel, A. V. (1992). The interpenetration of communicative contexts: Examples from medical encounters. In A. Duranti & C. Goodwin (Eds.), *Rethinking context: Language as an interactive phenomenon* (pp. 291–310). Cambridge, England: Cambridge University Press.

Cody, M., & McLaughlin, M. L. (Eds.). (1990). *The psychology of tactical communication.* London: Multilingual Matters.

Conley, J. M., & O'Barr, W. (1990). Rules versus relationships in small claims disputes. In A. D. Grimshaw (Ed.), *Conflict talk: Sociolinguistic investigations of arguments in conversations* (pp. 178–196). Cambridge, England: Cambridge University Press.

Coupland, N. (1988). Introduction: Towards a stylistics of discourse. In N. Coupland (Ed.), *Styles of discourse* (pp. 1–19). London: Croon Helm.

Coupland, N., Coupland, J., Giles, H., & Henwood, K. (1991). Intergenerational talk: Goal consonance and intergroup dissonance. In K. Tracy (Ed.), *Understanding face-to-face interaction: Issues linking goals and discourse* (pp. 79–100). Hillsdale, NJ: Erlbaum.

Craig, R. T. (1989). Communication as a practical discipline. In B. Dervin, L. Grossberg, B. J. O'Keefe, & E. Wartella (Eds.), *Rethinking communication: Vol. 1 Paradigm issues* (pp. 97–122). Newbury Park, CA: Sage.

Craig, R. T. (1992). Practical communication theory and the pragma–dialectical approach in conversation. In F. H. van Eemeren, R. Grootendorst, J. A. Blair, C. A. Willard (Eds.), *Argumentation illuminated* (pp. 51–61). Amsterdam: SISCSAT.

Craig, R. T. (1993, Summer). Why are there so *many* communication theories? *Journal of Communication, 43* (3), 26–33.

Craig, R. T. (1995). Applied communication research in a practical discipline. In K. Cissna (Ed.), *Applied communication in the twentieth century* (pp. 147–155). Mahwah, NJ: Erlbaum.

Craig, R. T., & Tracy, K. (1983). Introduction. In R. T. Craig & K. Tracy (Eds.), *Conversational coherence: Form, structure and strategy* (pp. 10–22). Beverly Hills, CA: Sage.

Craig, R. T., & Tracy, K. (1995). Grounded practical theory: The case of intellectual discussion. *Communication Theory, 5,* 258–272.

Craig, R. T., Tracy, K., & Spisak, F. (1986). The discourse of requests: Assessment of a politeness approach. *Human Communication Research, 12,* 437–468.

Dabbs, J. M. (1985). Temporal patterns of speech and gaze in social and intellectual conversation. In H. Giles & R. N. St Clair (Eds.), *Recent advances in language, communication and social psychology* (pp. 182–198). London: Erlbaum.

Davis, M. (1971). "That's interesting!" Towards a phenomenology of sociology and a sociology of phenomenology. *Philosophy of the Social Sciences, 1,* 309–344.

Dillon, G. L. (1991). *Contending rhetorics: Writing in academic disciplines.* Bloomington: University of Indiana Press.

Dillon, J. T. (1988). Questioning in education. In M. Meyer (Ed.), *Questions and questioning* (pp. 98–117). Berlin: Walter de Gruyer.

Duranti, A., & Goodwin, C. (Eds.). (1992). *Rethinking context:Language as an interactive phenomenon.* Cambridge, England: University of Cambridge Press.

Edwards, D., & Potter, J. (1992). *Discursive psychology.* London: Sage.

Eisenberg, E. M. (1984). Ambiguity as a strategy in organizational communication. *Communication Monographs, 51,* 227–242.

Fairclough, N. (1992). *Discourse and social change.* Cambridge, England: Polity Press.

Fisher, S., & Todd, A. D. (1986). Friendly persuasion: Negotiating decisions to use oral contraceptives. In S. Fisher & A. D. Todd (Eds.), *Discourse and institutional authority: Medicine, education and law* (pp. 3–25). Norwood, NJ: Ablex.

Fiske, J. (1991). Writing ethnographies: Contribution to a dialogue. *Quarterly Journal of Speech, 77,* 330–335.

Fitzgerald, T. K. (1993). *Metaphors of identity: A culture-communication dialogue.* Albany: State University of New York Press.

Fraser, B. (1990). Perspectives on politeness. *Journal of Pragmatics, 14,* 219–236.

Gadamer, H. (1984). *Truth and method.* New York: Crossroad Publishing.

Gaik, F. (1992). Radio talk–show therapy and the pragmatics of possible worlds. In A. Duranti & C. Goodwin (Eds.), *Rethinking context: Language as an interactive phenomenon* (pp. 217–289). Cambridge, England: University of Cambridge Press.

Gamson, W. A. (1992). *Talking politics.* Cambridge, England: Cambridge University Press.

Garfinkel, H. (1967). *Studies in ethnomethodology.* Englewood Cliffs, NJ: Prentice–Hall.

Geertz, C. (1984). "From the native's point of view": On the nature of anthropological understanding. In R. A. Shweder & R. A. LeVine (Eds.), *Culture theory: Essays on mind, self, and emotion* (pp. 123–136). Cambridge, England: Cambridge University Press.

Gergen, K. J. (1994). The limits of pure critique. In H. W. Simons & M. Billig (Eds.), *Postmodernism: Reconstructing ideology critique* (pp. 58–78). London: Sage.

Gilbert, G. N., & Mulkay, M. (1984). *Opening Pandora's box: A sociological analysis of scientists' discourse.* Cambridge, England: Cambridge University Press.

Goffman, E. (1955). On facework: An analysis of ritual elements in social interaction. *Psychiatry, 18,* 213–231.

Goffman, E. (1959). *The presentation of self in everyday life.* New York: Anchor Books.

Goffman, E. (1981). *Forms of talk.* Philadelphia: University of Pennsylvania Press.

Graesser, A. C. (1990). Psychological research on question answering and question asking. *Discourse Processes, 13,* 259–260.

Greene, J. O., Lindsey, A. E., & Hawn, J. J. (1990). Social goals and speech production: Effects of multiple goals on pausal phenomena. *Journal of Language and Social Psychology, 9,* 119–134.

Grimshaw, A. (1989). *Collegial discourse: Professional conversation among peers.* Norwood, NJ: Ablex.

Grimshaw, A. (Ed.). (1994). *What's going on here?* Norwood, NJ: Ablex.

Gumperz, J. J. (Ed.). (1982a). *Language and social identity.* Cambridge, England: Cambridge University Press

Gumperz, J. J. (1982b). *Discourse strategies.* Cambridge, England: Cambridge University Press.

Habermas, J. (1979). *Communication and the evolution of society.* (T. McCarthy, Trans.) Boston: Beacon Press.

Harre, R. (Ed.). (1987). *The social construction of emotions.* Oxford, England: Blackwell.

Heath, S. B. (1983). *Ways with words: Language, life, and work in communities and classrooms.* Cambridge, England: Cambridge University Press.

Heritage, J. (1995). *'Oh' prefaced responses to inquiry.* Paper presented at the Georgetown Linguistics Society Conference on Developments in Discourse Analysis, Washington, D.C.

Hewitt, J. P., & Stokes, R. (1975). Disclaimers. *American Sociological Review, 40,* 1–11.

Hill, J. H., & Irvine, J. T. (Eds.). (1993). *Responsibility and evidence in oral discourse.* Cambridge, England: Cambridge University Press.

Hodge, R., & Kress, G. (1993). *Language as ideology* (2nd ed.). London: Routledge.

Hunkins, F. P. (1989). *Teaching thinking through effective questioning.* Boston, MA: Christopher–Gordon.

Hymes. D. (1974). *Foundations in sociolinguistics: An ethnographic approach.* Philadelphia: University of Pennsylvania Press.

Jablin, F. M., & Miller, V. D. (1990). Interviewer and applicant questioning behavior in employment interviews. *Management Communication Quarterly, 4,* 51–86.

Jaworski, A. (1994). Apologies and non–apologies: Negotiations in speech act realization. *Text, 14,* 185–206.

Johnson, M. (1987). *The body in the mind: The bodily basis of meaning, imagination and reason.* Chicago: University of Chicago Press.

Kaplan, A. (1964). *The conduct of inquiry.* San Francisco: Chandler.

Katriel, T. (1986). *Talking straight: Dugri speech in Israeli Sabra culture.* Cambridge, England: Cambridge University Press.

Kaufer, D. S., & Geisler, C. (1989). Novelty in academic writing. *Written Communication, 6,* 286–311.

Keppler, A., & Luckmann, T. (1991). 'Teaching': Conversational transmission of knowledge. In I. Markova & K. Foppa (Eds.), *Asymmetries in dialogue* (pp. 143–165). Hertfordshire, England: Harvester Wheatsheaf.

Knapp. M. L. (1979). *Social intercourse: From greeting to goodbye.* Boston: Allyn & Bacon.

Knoblauch, H. (1991). The taming of foes: The avoidance of asymmetry in informal discussions. In I. Markova & K. Foppa (Eds.), *Asymmetries in dialogue* (pp. 166–194). Hertfordshire, England: Harvester Wheatsheaf.

Knorr–Cetina, K. D. (1981). *The manufacture of knowledge.* Oxford, England: Pergamon Press.

Kochman, T. (1981). *Black and white styles in conflict.* Chicago: University of Chicago Press.

Kuo, S–L. (1994). Agreement and disagreement strategies in radio conversation. *Research on Language and Social Interaction, 27,* 95–121.

Labov, W., & Fanshel, D (1977). *Therapeutic discourse: Psychotherapy as conversation.* New York: Academic Press.

Lakoff, G. (1987). *Women, fire, and dangerous things: What categories reveal about the mind.* Chicago: University of Chicago Press.

Lakoff, G., & Johnson, M. (1980). *Metaphors we live by.* Chicago: University of Chicago Press.

Lakoff, R. T. (1990). *Talking power.* New York: Basic Books.

Latour, B., & Woolgar, S. (1986). *Laboratory life: The construction of scientific facts.* Princeton, NJ: Princeton University Press.

Lehnert, W. G. (1978). *The process of question answering.* Hillsdale, NJ: Erlbaum.

Levy, M. R., & Gurevitch, M. (1994). *Defining communication studies: Reflections on the future of the field.* Oxford, England: Oxford University Press.

Lim, T., & Bowers, J. W. (1991). Facework, solidarity, approbation and tact. *Human Communication Research, 17,* 415–450.

Linde, C. (1988). The quantitative study of communicative success: Politeness and accidents in aviation discourse. *Language in Society, 17,* 375–399.

Linnell, P., & Jonsson, L. (1991). Suspect stories: Perspective setting in an asymmetrical situation. In I. Markova & K. Foppa (Eds.), *Asymmetries in dialogue* (pp. 75–100). Hertfordshire, England: Wheatsheaf.

Lynch, M. (1985). *Art and artifact in laboratory sciences.* London: Routledge & Kegan Paul.

Manzo, J. F. (1993). Jurors' narratives of personal experience in deliberative talk. *Text, 13,* 267–290.

Maynard, D. W. (1984). *Inside plea bargaining.* New York: Plenum.

McKinlay, A., & Potter, J. (1987). Model discourse: Interpretative repertoires in scientists' conference talk. *Social Studies of Science, 17,* 443–463.

Mead, G. H. (1934). *Mind, self and society.* Chicago: University of Chicago Press.

Mehan, H. (1986). The role of language and the language of role in institutional decision–making. In S. Fisher & A. D. Todd (Eds.), *Discourse and institutional authority: Medicine, education and law* (pp. 140–163). Norwood, NJ: Ablex.

Michaels, S., & Collins, J. (1984). Oral discourse styles: Classroom interaction and the acquisition of literacy. In D. Tannen (Ed.), *Coherence in spoken and written discourse* (pp. 219–244). Norwood, NJ: Ablex.

Mishler, E. (1986). *Research interviewing: Context and narrative.* Cambridge: Harvard University Press.

Moore, C. M. (1994). Why do we mediate? In J. P. Folger & T. S. Jones (Eds.), *New directions in mediation: Communication research and perspectives.* Newbury Park, CA: Sage.

Myers, G. (1989). The pragmatics of politeness in scientific articles. *Applied Linguistics, 10,* 1–35.

Myers, G. (1990). *Writing biology.* Madison: University of Wisconsin Press.

Ochs, E. (1979). Transcription as theory. In E. Ochs & B. Schieffelin (Eds.), *Developmental pragmatics* (pp. 43–72). New York: Academic Press.

Ochs, E. (1993). Constructing social identity: A language socialization perspective. *Research on Language and Social Interaction, 26,* 287–306.

Ochs, E., Taylor, C., Rudolph, D., & Smith, R. (1992). Storytelling as a theory–building activity. *Discourse Processes, 15,* 37–72.

Orr, C. J. (1980). Reporters confront the president: Sustaining a counterpoised situation. *Quarterly Journal of Speech, 66,* 17–32.

Pavlidou, T. (1991). Cooperation and the choice of linguistic means: Some evidence from the use of the subjunctive in modern Greek. *Journal of Pragmatics, 15,* 11–42.

Pearce, W. B. (1994). Recovering agency. In S. Deetz (Ed.), *Communication yearbook 17* (pp. 34–54). Thousand Oaks, CA: Sage.

Pelz, D. C., & Andrews, F. M. (1976). *Scientists in organizations: Productive climates for research and development* (Rev. ed.). Ann Arbor, MI: Institute for Social Research.

Penman, R. (1987). Discourse in courts: Cooperation, coercion, and coherence. *Discourse Processes, 10,* 210–218.

Penman, R. (1990). Facework and politeness: Multiple goals in courtroom discourse. *Journal of Language and Social Psychology, 9,* 15–38.

Penman, R. (1991). Goals, games, and moral orders: A paradoxical case in court? In K. Tracy (Ed.), *Understanding face-to-face interaction: Issues linking goals and discourse* (pp. 21–42). Hillsdale, NJ: Erlbaum.

Philips, S. (1983). *The invisible culture: Communication in classroom and community on the Warm Springs Indian Reservation.* New York: Longman.

Philipsen, G. (1990). Speaking "like a man" in Teamsterville: Cultural patterns of role enactment in an urban neighborhood. In D. Carbaugh (Ed.), *Cultural communication and intercultural contact* (pp. 11–20). Hillsdale, NJ: Erlbaum.

Philipsen, G. (1991). Two issues in the evaluation of ethnographic studies of communicative practices. *Quarterly Journal of Speech, 77,* 327–39.

Pomerantz, A. (1988). Offering a candidate answer: An information–seeking strategy. *Communication Monographs, 55,* 360–373.

Potter, J. (1984). Testability, flexibility: Kuhnian values in scientists' discourse concerning theory choice. *Philosophy of the Social Sciences, 14,* 303–330.

Potter, J., & Wetherell, M. (1987). *Discourse and social psychology.* London: Sage.

Ragan, S. L. (1990). Verbal play and multiple goals in the gynaecological exam interaction. *Journal of Language and Social Psychology 9,* 61–78.

Rawlins, W. (1989). A dialectical analysis of the tensions, functions and strategic challenges of communication in young adult friendships. In J. Anderson (Ed.), *Communication yearbook 12* (pp. 157–189). Newbury Park, CA: Sage.

Rawlins, W. (1991). On enacting friendship and interrogating discourse. In K. Tracy (Ed.), *Understanding face-to-face interaction: Linking goals and discourse* (pp. 101–115). Hillsdale, NJ: Erlbaum.

Rorty, R. (1989). *Contingency, irony, and solidarity.* Cambridge, England: Cambridge University Press.

Ross, M., & Fletcher, G. J. O. (1985). Attribution and social perception. In G. Lindsey & E. Aronson (Eds.), *Handbook of social psychology: Volume II. Special fields and applications* (pp.73–122). New York: Random House.

Rumelhart. M. A. (1983). When in doubt: Strategies used in response to interactional uncertainty. *Discourse Processes, 6,* 377–402.

Sanders, R. E., & Sigman, S. J. (1994). An editorial caveat. *Research on Language and Social Interaction, 27,* 419–421.

Sands, R. G. (1993). "Can you overlap here?" A question for an interdisciplinary team. *Discourse Processes, 16,* 545–564.

Sapir, E. (1949). Papers by Sapir reprinted in D. Mandelbaum (Ed.), *Selected writing of Edward Sapir.* Berkeley: University of California Press.

Schegloff, E. (1979). Identification and recognition in telephone conversation openings. In G. Psathas (Ed.), *Everyday language: Studies in ethnomethodology* (pp. 23–78). New York: Irvington Press.

Schegloff, E. (1989). From interview to confrontation. Observations on the Bush/Rather encounter. *Research on Language and Social Interaction, 22,* 215–240.

Schegloff, E. (1992). In another context. In A. Duranti & C. Goodwin (Eds.), *Rethinking context: Language as an interactive phenomenon* (pp. 191–227). Cambridge, England: Cambridge University Press.

Schiffrin, D. (1987). *Discourse markers.* Cambridge, England: Cambridge University Press.

Schiffrin, D. (1993). "Speaking for another" in sociolinguistic interviews: Alignments, identities and frames. In D. Tannen (Ed.), *Framing in discourse* (pp. 231–263). Oxford, England: Oxford University Press.

Schiffrin, D. (1994). *Approaches to discourse*. Oxford, England: Blackwell.

Scott, M. B., & Lyman, S. (1968). Accounts. *American Sociological Review, 33*, 46–62.

Scotton, C. M. (1985). What the heck, sir: Style shifting and lexical colouring as features of powerful language. In R. L. Street, Jr., & J. N. Cappella (Eds.), *Sequence and pattern in communicative behaviour*. London: Edward Arnold.

Seibold, D. R., & Spitzberg, B. H. (1982). Attributional theory and research: Review and implications for communication. In B. J. Dervin & M. J. Voight (Eds.), *Progress in communication sciences* (Vol. 3, pp. 85–125). Norwood, NJ: Ablex.

Semin, G. R., & Manstead, A. S. R. (1983). *The accountability of conduct*. New York: Academic Press.

Shotter, J. (1993). *Conversational realities: Constructing life through language*. London: Sage.

Shotter, J., & Gergen, K. J. (Eds.) (1989). *Texts of identity*, London: Sage.

Shotter, J., & Gergen, K. J. (1994). Social construction: Knowledge, self, others, and continuing the conversation. In S. Deetz (Ed.), *Communication yearbook 17* (pp. 3–33). Thousand Oaks, CA: Sage.

Sifianou, M. (1989). On the telephone again! Differences in telephone behaviour: England versus Greece. *Language in Society, 18*, 527–544.

Simons, H. W. (1970). Requirements, problems and strategies: A theory of persuasion for social movements. *Quarterly Journal of Speech, 56*, 1–11.

Sinclair, J. McH., & Coulthard, R. M. (1975). *Towards an analysis of discourse: The English used by teachers and pupils*. Oxford: Oxford University Press.

Soyland, A. J. (1994). Functions of the psychiatric case summary. *Text, 14*, 113–140.

Swales, J. M. (1990). *Genre analysis: English in academic and research settings*. Cambridge, England: Cambridge University Press.

Tannen, D. (1984). *Conversational style: Analyzing talk among friends*. Norwood, NJ: Ablex.

Tannen, D. (1989) *Talking voices*. Cambridge, England: Cambridge University Press.

Tannen, D. (1993). What's in a frame? Surface evidence for underlying expectations. In D. Tannen (Ed.), *Framing in discourse* (pp. 14–56). Oxford, England: Oxford University Press.

Tannen, D., & Wallet, C. (1993). Interactive frames and knowledge schemas in interaction: Examples from a medical examination/interview. In D. Tannen (Ed.), *Framing in discourse* (pp. 57–76). Oxford, England: Oxford University Press.

Taylor, T. J. (1992). *Mutual misunderstandings: Scepticism and the theorizing of language and interpretation*. Durham, NC: Duke University Press.

Tedeschi, J. T. (1990). Self presentation and social influence: An interactionist perspective. In M. J. Cody & M. J. McLaughlin (Eds.), *The psychology of tactical communication* (pp. 301–323). Clevedon, England: Multilingual Matters.

Ting–Toomey, S. (Ed.). (1994). *The challenge of facework.* Albany: State University of New York Press.

Tracy, K. (1984). The effect of multiple goals on conversational relevance and topic shift. *Communication Monographs, 51,* 274–287.

Tracy, K. (1988). A discourse analysis of four discourse studies. *Discourse Processes, 11,* 243–259.

Tracy, K. (1990). The many faces of facework. In H. Giles & P. Robinson (Eds.), *Handbook of language and social psychology* (pp. 209–226). Chichester, England: Wiley.

Tracy, K. (Ed.). (1991). *Understanding face-to-face interaction: Issues linking goals and discourse.* Hillsdale, NJ: Erlbaum.

Tracy, K. (1994). Boundary drawing in language and social interaction study. *Research on Language and Social Interaction, 27,* 423–425.

Tracy, K. (1995a). Action–implicative discourse analysis. *Journal of Language and Social Psychology, 14,* 195–215.

Tracy, K. (1995b). How should academics talk about ideas? *Proceedings of the ninth SCA/AFA conference on argumentation* (pp. 326–334), Annandale, VA: Speech Communication Association.

Tracy, K., & Baratz, S. (1993). Intellectual discussion in the academy as situated discourse. *Communication Monographs, 60,* 300–320.

Tracy, K., & Carjuzaa, J. (1993). Identity enactment in intellectual discussion. *Journal of Language and Social Psychology, 12,* 171–194.

Tracy, K., & Coupland, N. (1990). Multiple goals in discourse: An overview of issues. *Journal of Language and Social Psychology, 9,* 1–13.

Tracy, K., & Muller, N. (1994). Talking about ideas: Academics' beliefs about appropriate communicative practices. *Research on Language and Social Interaction, 27,* 319–349.

Tracy, K., & Naughton, J. (1994). The identity work of questioning in intellectual discussion. *Communication Monographs, 61,* 281–302.

Tracy, K., & Spradlin, A. (1994). "Talking like a mediator": Conversational moves of experienced divorce mediators. In J. P. Folger & T. S. Jones (Eds.), *New directions in mediation: Communication research and perspectives* (pp. 110–132). Thousand Oaks, CA: Sage.

van Dijk, T. A. (1987). *Communicating racism: Ethnic prejudice in thought and talk.* Newbury Park, CA: Sage.

van Dijk, T. A. (1993). Principles of critical discourse analysis. *Discourse and Society, 4,* 249–283.

van Eemeren, F. H., & Grootendorst, R. (1984). *Speech acts in argumentative discussions: A theoretical model for the analysis of discussions directed toward solving conflicts of opinion.* Dordrecht, Holland: Foris Publications.

van Eemeren, F. H., Grootendorst, R., Jackson, S., & Jacobs, S. (1993). *Reconstructing argumentative discourse.* Tucaloosa: University of Alabama Press.

Verhoeven, J. C. (1993). An interview with Erving Goffman, 1980. *Research on Language and Social Interaction, 26,* 317–348.

Walker, A. G. (1986). The verbatim record: Myth and the reality. In S. Fisher & A. D. Todd (Eds.), *Discourse and institutional authority: Medicine, education and law* (pp. 205–222). Norwood, NJ: Ablex.

Walton, D. N. (1989). *Question-reply argumentation.* New York: Greenwood Press.

Werner, C. M., & Baxter, L.A. (1994). Temporal qualities of relationships: Organismic, transactional, and dialectical views. In M. L. Knapp. & G. R. Miller (Eds.), *Handbook of interpersonal communication* (pp. 323–379). Thousand Oaks, CA: Sage.

Whorf, B L. (1956). *Language, thought and reality.* Cambridge, MA: MIT Press.

Wilson, S. (1992). Face and facework in negotiation. In L. L. Putnam & M. E. Roloff (Eds.), *Communication and negotiation* (pp. 176–205). Newbury Park, CA: Sage.

Wood, L. A., & Kroger, R. O. (1994). The analysis of facework in discourse: Review and proposal. *Journal of Language and Social Psychology, 13,* 248–277.

Woodbury, H. (1984). The strategic use of questions in court. *Semiotica, 48,* 197–228.

Yahya–Othman, S. (1994). Covering one's social back: Politeness among the Swahili. *Text, 14* 141–161.

Author Index

Subject Index